What a staggering realization:
Jesus came to the world *WE* live in.

If we are to be children of God in our world, we have to function in an atmosphere of distractions, disappointments, and defeats.

It isn't easy for us to understand that if we are to follow Christ at all, it will have to be on a day like today, in a world like this one.

We trudge along waiting for another time and another place. He is with us and we do not recognize Him. While we watch the distant horizon for His entry, He is standing beside us.

Don't miss the next Young Adult Book available March, 1977

Return to Identity
by Wes Reagan

Return to Identity concludes the study of Jesus' life and offers practical wisdom drawn from the book of James.

Return to Identity reminds you that becoming like Christ is not a matter of coasting casually along until one day you have the unexpected opportunity to be a Christian hero. Christianity is not a self-help project. It is a response to the gift of God in Christ. In our return to our Father we find the truest expression of our own identity.

Be sure to read these chapters:
"We Have It Backwards"
"The Strangest Parable"
"A Boy's Freedom and a Father's Love"
"Eye of the Storm"
"Don't Look in the Cemetery"
"The Corpse"

WHAT ARE WE WAITING FOR?

Jesus Is Here

**by
Wes Reagan**

Obtain a 40-page leader's guide to accompany this paperback. Order number 1963 from Standard Publishing or your local supplier.

A Division of Standard Publishing
Cincinnati, Ohio 45231
No. 40032

Scripture quotations are taken from the *Revised Standard Version,* © 1946 and 1952, unless otherwise noted.

KJV—*King James Version* of 1611.
NAS—*New American Standard Bible.* © The Lockman Foundation, 1963.
NIV—*The New International Version.* © 1973 by New York Bible Society International.
NEB—*The New English Bible.* © the Delegates of the Oxford University Press and the Syndics of the Cambridge University Press, 1961, 1970.

Chapter themes based on International Bible Lessons for Christian Teaching, © 1973 by the Lesson Committee.
© 1976, The STANDARD PUBLISHING Company,
a division of Standex International Corp.

Library of Congress Catalog No. 75-44589
ISBN 0-87239-061-6

Printed in U.S.A. 1976

Table of Contents

 1 Coming Soon: The Unique 7
 2 Can You Celebrate? 14
 3 On a Day Like Today 21
 4 Dream Come True 28
 5 Perfect—at First, at Last 35
 6 A Life's Work Launched 42
 7 The Waiting Is Over 49
 8 Called to Discipleship 55
 9 Impostor Exposed 62
10 Authentic Power 69
11 The Intruder 76
12 Lord, Give Me an Aspirin 83
13 Mandate to Love 90

1

Coming Soon: The Unique

When God reveals himself to us, He gives us an insight into the nature of reality. This is true because His nature is that which constitutes reality. Therefore when we know more about God we know more about the world we live in. More importantly, when we know more about Him we know more about ourselves. The narrative of Luke 1:26-38 tells a remarkable story of the revelation of God to Mary. As we come to understand this story better we will come to understand ourselves better also.

Chosen

"The angel Gabriel was sent from God to a city of Galilee named Nazareth, to a virgin betrothed to a man whose name was Joseph, of the house of David; and the

---

Scripture Resource: Luke 1:26-38

virgin's name was Mary'' (Luke 1:26, 27). Note how careful the choosing of God is. Gabriel was sent to a particular town in a particular province. He was sent to a particular young woman who was betrothed to a specific young man. Of all the women in the world, Gabriel was told to go to the Mary who was betrothed to Joseph.

The fact that Mary was singled out by God to become the mother of Jesus teaches us some very important lessons. One is that God does have plans and aspirations for our lives. Not only is it all right for us to be true to our own nature, it is necessary that we be. God does not simply allow us to be ourselves. He insists that we be. He has a purpose for us that nobody else is prepared to fulfill. Should you become an imitation of another, the world would be deprived of the genuine you.

Another lesson is that you do not need to be at the nerve center of the world in order to be involved in God's work. God will find you even if you live in Muddy Gap, Wyoming, or Tallulah Falls, Georgia. Nazareth was not exactly the crossroads of the world, and Joseph was not the mayor. When the Lord needed Mary He found her.

As Mary was chosen of God, so you also are chosen of God. God is just as personally and just as specifically involved in your life as in hers. God loves you and has chosen to work through you.

Troubled

When Gabriel told Mary that she was greatly favored by the Lord she was troubled. Watching from a spectator's point of view, we would expect her to be elated at the news that the Lord had chosen her. When we put ourselves in her place, however, the perspective changes.

If *I* were a young Jewish girl engaged to be married and an angel appeared to *me* telling me that *I* was especially chosen of God, *I* would be very frightened. What does this mean? What is expected of me? How will my life be changed? Will I be able to live up to expectations?

To be called of God is often not a peaceful experience. It is sometimes frightening, sometimes confusing. It often arouses feelings of uncertainty as to whether I can live up to the call or not. God may expect decisions and commitments of me that I am not sure I am ready to make. I may fear that I am not even capable of making them. Such a call identifies me with other people who have done great things for God. How could I not live up to their examples?

The spectator is inclined to think how nice it would be to have the recognition and the sense of having an important mission. But the person who actually receives the call tends more to think of responsibilities and expectations that are involved in being chosen of God.

The Announcement

Sensing Mary's distress, the angel gently told her that she need not be afraid. Then he made to Mary the announcement the world had waited on since Adam and Eve had been expelled from Eden. "You will conceive in your womb and bear a son, and you shall call his name

Jesus," Gabriel said (Luke 1:31).

The angel went ahead to say that this son would be no ordinary son. He would be the Son of God and would be an eternal king.

How could Mary keep from being afraid? From obscurity she was vaulted abruptly into the center of the stage of God's purpose for mankind. The only reason that she needed not be afraid is that the God who calls also provides. God would make her equal to the demands of the calling He gave her.

Imagine you are suddenly catapulted into a central and conspicuous place in order to serve God. Perhaps it is necessary for you to be the spokesman for racial justice or honest government. Perhaps you need to perform some significant act of service to someone who badly needs help. Perhaps you will be the one who holds a position of power and influence; you must make critical decisions that affect the lives of others.

How can you keep from being afraid? Of course, the butterflies in the stomach that accompany any great exhilaration probably cannot and should not be avoided. The larger underlying fears, however, are made manageable by the knowledge that God will make you a big enough man or woman for the task He has called you to do. The God who calls also provides.

Mary did not have any idea how Gabriel's announcement could possibly come true. Yet her lack of awareness of God's method was no handicap for God. The announcement did come true. Mary was equal to the task.

The Problem

"How can I have a baby when I have no husband?" Mary asked. This was not the naive question of one who did not understand the birth process. Mary understood it well enough. She knew that babies were not conceived in a rich imagination. The angel was promising that she, as a virgin, would give birth to a son. *This,* she said, *is more than I can understand.*

Two things are striking about Mary's comment. One is her total honesty. Though understandably awestruck at speaking with an angel, she blurted out her very candid reaction to the angel's promise, "A woman cannot have a baby by herself." It was in the context of this beautiful honesty that God was able to work the miracle of all miracles.

Mary's comment is also noteworthy in the extent to which it identifies with us. How often do we feel that there is no point in praying about something because we feel it couldn't be changed anyway? How often do we hesitate to trust God because we cannot personally see any way out of our problem? Mary did not try to protect God from an impossible situation, but responded honestly to Him. She trusted Him for what she found impossible. We should trust God enough to leave open the possibility of His working even in situations that seem impossible to us.

The Solution

Mary treated the problem seriously and responded to God honestly. The angel, in turn, answered with the work of the Spirit and the power of God. With God nothing is impossible. In the light of our experience about babies being born, this is hard to understand. In the light of God's creation of the entire human family and of life itself, it is not so difficult to see. God created Adam and Eve without any human parents at all. God created the birth process through which all children except Jesus have been born. God acted in unusual ways to bring about the birth of Isaac when Isaac's father was one hundred years old and his mother was ninety. In that case God opened a previously dead womb to bring a special child into being. God also acted in an unusual way to bring John the Baptist into being.

The God who created Adam and Eve, the God who created the birth process, and the God who opened dead wombs could certainly bring a child into the world without a human father if He chose to do so. The God who did the unusual could also do the unique.

The work of the Spirit and the power of God can overcome barricades which seem insurmountable to the human eye. In fact, the uniqueness of the birth of Christ testifies that He is uniquely the Son of God. "The Holy Spirit will come upon you, and the power of the Most High will overshadow you; therefore the child to be born will be called holy, the Son of God" (Luke 1:35). This gospel is not simply saying that God *could* cause Jesus to be born of a virgin. It is saying that God *deliberately* caused Jesus to be born in this manner in order that we might recognize the absolute uniqueness of His sonship.

What Mary saw to be a problem, God saw to be an affirmation. Here is the difference between the human and the divine perspective. We see burdens and dead end streets. God sees opportunities and broad avenues of love and service. Where we anticipate defeat God envisions an even larger victory. Where we are caught up in feelings of our own weakness, God is rich in the awareness of His strength. The work of the Spirit and the power of God will overcome obstacles in our lives just as they overcame that which Mary saw to be a problem.

The Handmaid of the Lord

What is it that makes it possible for God to work in the life of an otherwise defeated human being? Mary could not have received the promise if she had not looked beyond the problem. Why was the situation not stalemated at that point?

The thing that opened Mary's life to God's miracle was her attitude of trusting submission. She said, "I am the handmaid of the Lord; let it be to me according to your word" (Luke 1:38). What magnificent faith! She told

God, "I am yours to do with as you will." She signed a blank check for her total being. That is what made Mary such a useful servant of God.

It is easy for us to underestimate the enormous commitment Mary was making. Remember that she was still a very young woman. Remember that this occurred at a time in history when women just did not occupy prominent or leading roles. Remember that Mary had just been the recipient of an awesome promise from Gabriel. Even in the light of these staggering considerations, Mary was still able to say to God, "Whatever you are calling me to is fine." With this kind of trust Mary displayed the quality that led God to her.

God is just as eager to pour rich blessings into your life as He was to bless Mary. The only thing that can hinder the coming of these blessings is your reluctance to open your life to Him. If you trust God greatly and are able to pray with real meaning, "I am Yours to do with as You will," God will flood your life with blessings beyond your greatest imagination. Mary would never have supposed that she would be the mother of the Christ. Like Mary, you are not able to dream of the purposes God can fulfill in your life if you are open to Him.

2

Can You Celebrate?

A friend recently said to me, "I didn't learn much about how to celebrate as I was growing up." It is regrettable when this important dimension of life is not developed. Sometimes people not only don't know how, but they would feel vaguely guilty about it if they did. They have absorbed the concept that religion must be a somber matter. Nothing could be further from the truth.

One of the great celebration passages in the Bible is the song of Mary in Luke 1. In elation of spirit Mary begins,

"My soul magnifies the Lord,
and my spirit rejoices in God my Savior,
for he has regarded the low estate of his
  handmaiden,

Scripture Resource: Luke 1:39-55

> For behold, henceforth all generations will
> call me blessed;
> for he who is mighty has done great things for me,
> and holy is his name'' (Luke 1:46-49).

The fact that almighty God is doing great things cries out to be celebrated. God is great in mercy, strong in power. He is able to conquer the arrogant and the mighty, but He raises the humble and satisfies the hungry. He has not forgotten His people. What greater reason for celebration could there possibly be? It is well past time for joyless religion to be abandoned. Let there be gladness and singing and praise. Let us learn again to celebrate the mighty acts of God.

God's Celebrating People

Since ancient times the people of God have been celebrating people. The Passover celebration was an observance of the time God protected the Israelites from the tenth plague and delivered them from the slavery of Egypt. During the week of the Passover the Israelites did many things to help recreate the spirit of deliverance. They ate unleavened bread because that was the type of bread that Israel took with them into the wilderness. They offered a lamb as a sacrifice and ate of its meat with bitter herbs remembering their hasty departure and bitter bondage. That was and still is repeated by many Jews each year to commemorate the work of God.

The feast of Pentecost occurred fifty days after the Passover. Loaves of unleavened bread were offered signifying the first products of the harvest. Celebration of this annual feast bound the Jewish people together. In the Christian heritage this is remembered as the occasion of the coming of the Holy Spirit (Acts 2).

The feast of the Tabernacles was a celebration remembering God's care for Israel during the time of the wilderness wanderings. When people experienced the working of God in their lives they wanted to preserve that in their memory. Because they did this consistently, their year became a series of celebrations remembering how God was active and gracious in their lives.

When Mary sang her song of praise to God, she was honoring an ancient and hallowed tradition. Her praise was the expression of her elation of spirit in the face of God's gift. How appropriate that the greatest act of God, the giving of Christ, is marked by this exquisite song of praise and thanksgiving.

Why Celebrate?

Although we are familiar with the celebrative feeling, perhaps we need to better understand the spiritual significance of celebration. Why did the father of the prodigal son announce a party to celebrate his son's homecoming (Luke 15:11-32)? Why is it appropriate for us to have a sense of celebration as we take communion, enjoy fellowship, or talk with others about what God is doing in our lives?

Celebration underlines significance. Hundreds of things happen every day that are routine, expected, and relatively unimportant. They do not need to be celebrated. In fact, if all of them were celebrated, celebration would lose its meaning. Celebration marks that which is of unusual worth or importance. If it is made commonplace, there is no way to designate superior value. The regular pay check is received with appreciation. The unexpected bonus is received with celebration. Every day of life is important, but your birthday is a day of special celebration. So it is with Mother's Day, Father's Day, and other days set aside to signify the special importance of certain people or events.

Celebration is also an aid to memory. With the passing of years and generations, very significant things fade in memory. The printing press was a revolutionary invention, but we have come to take it so much for granted that we have lost much of the awareness of how much it af-

"What are we celebrating? Today is the anniversary of my first successful chocolate cake!"

fects our lives. The same is true of electricity, radio, television, the telephone, and modern transportation. In spite of the fact that the first space travel occurred fairly recently, we have lost much of the sense of awe and wonder we experienced at the first.

It is natural for events to recede in our memory as we get further from them. That is a blessing when it allows pain and sorrow to become less piercing and burdensome. It means, however, that we have to give special attention to things that we want to remain strong in our memory. We celebrate birthdays as one way of affirming the significance of personhood. A birthday is that one time of year when we say to a person, "We may often seem to take you for granted, but we love you and you are special to us."

Celebration is also important because it provides for

the adequate expression of our more profound feelings. We may be a little like the man who said, "Sometimes I am so overwhelmed with how much my wife means to me I can scarcely refrain from telling her."

It is easy to talk of surface things. It is not easy to talk of that which is too deep for words and too great a treasure to be exposed to the common view. That is why we need vehicles to express those "too large for words" feelings that we have. Celebration meets that need.

Life Without Celebration

What happens when a person cannot celebrate? What effect does it have on a life not to be able to express its deepest feelings?

When a person has no capacity for celebration, he will know facts but will not understand significance. He will be capable of condemning or defending but will not be able to weigh values. He can distinguish between right and wrong but has difficulty telling the difference between the lesser and the greater good. His life might have correctness, but it cannot have a good sense of priorities. In short, his world will be marked by a shallow sense of technical correctness which masks a profound lack of understanding of its meaning. He will have the letter of the gospel, but not the spirit.

If a person does not celebrate, he forgets. It has been said that those who do not study history are doomed to repeat it. I heard a seminary professor say there has been no new heresy since the second century. Everything that has disturbed the unity of churches has happened before, often hundreds of times before. How blessed we would be if we would celebrate regularly and vigorously the great acts of God in delivering His people. Then we would not have to lapse into apostasy with its pain and lostness.

Life without celebration is inhibiting and frustrating. When our great feelings are repressed, we cannot be happy and often make others unhappy as well. Instead of being chronic critics, let us be rejoicing Christians, celebrating the fact that God has done and is doing remarkable things in the world and in our lives.

Celebrations That Do Not Celebrate

There are some warnings in the Scriptures that warn against allowing celebrations to become meaningless rituals. Acts of celebration become hollow when they are separated from their significance. Amos wrote of the irony of rituals when a true relationship with God did not exist. He accused the people of Israel of only going through the motions of worship while they were oppressing the poor (Amos 4:1-5). They had lost the meaning of the celebration. The ritual was meaningless. The proper things were done, but the meaning was not there.

Paul talks about a similar problem in regard to the Lord's Supper in 1 Corinthians 11. It is possible to eat and drink without discerning the body of Christ. When this is done the eating and drinking is meaningless. It is a judgment upon those who mock the meaning by partaking meaninglessly.

It is possible to put so much emphasis on the *what* of the Lord's Supper that we forget about the *why* of it. When that happens it fails to serve the purpose for which Jesus instituted it. Many would be incensed if the Lord's Supper were omitted, but could eat it thoughtlessly and routinely without being disturbed.

While the celebrative dimension is important to the Christian life, we need to be careful not to mistake the symbol for the substance. We need to stay centered on the actions of God rather than on our means of celebrating those acts.

Mary's Celebration

Mary's celebration was her response to the greatest of all of God's acts. As we think about some of the things

God has done, we are impressed with the significance of that act. We are talking about the God who acted in creation. He *spoke* the world into existence and graced it with form and beauty. He created all the remarkable systems that allow the interrelationship between the various kinds of life. He made man in His own image and filled man with His Spirit. Mary was celebrating an even greater act than this.

Mary was celebrating the fact that in her womb was the Son of God. She had conceived by the power of the Holy Spirit, and her child was to be uniquely God's Son. She had been chosen to have an essential part in God's ultimate revelation of himself to man. Is it any wonder that her soul magnified the Lord? Is it not a wonder, rather, that any soul can refrain from magnifying the Lord as he considers such magnificent news?

There are many today who celebrate God's act in Christ. In worship and in acts of love and service they find ways to express to God their praise and thanksgiving. They are not somber, strained, worried Christians who spend most of their time fearing they will be lost for doing something wrong. They are smiling, rejoicing, and singing Christians, who spend most of their time celebrating the limitless blessings of God. Their biggest problem is not knowing how to find adequate means of expressing to Him the joy and gratitude of their hearts.

3

On a Day Like Today

We have to keep reminding ourselves that Jesus came to the world we live in. This baby who was born in a stable and laid in a feeding trough for animals was the Lord coming physically into the real world. The beauty, strength, and courage of His life did not exist on a sheltered stage. They existed in real life, in the midst of a very complicated and frustrating world.

The impact of this realization is that if we are to be children of God in our world we have to function in an atmosphere of distractions, disappointments, and defeats. Our splendid idealism that waits until conditions are favorable is a dream. Our present call is not to be children of God in Heaven but in the world. We are to be an expression of God's love in a world of sin, disap-

---

Scripture Resource: Luke 2:7-20

pointment, not feeling up-to-par, distractions, frustrations, bad weather, opposition, self-doubt, weariness, and apathy.

This is a staggering realization. Let's imagine just some of the factors involved in an ordinary family situation.

Joe's World

Joe Sanders is a forty year-old husband and father. Joe's business is not as good as it was last year. Expenses are up. Joe has made commitments on the basis of previous income. It was natural that he should do that. Since he started working twenty years ago he has managed to make more money each year than he did the previous year. He was blind to the possibility that it would not always be this way.

Joe is tired a lot. He doesn't have the unflagging energy he used to. It is more of a temptation to let things slide, to do them later, or to do them less carefully. Especially Joe does not feel like coming in from a day's work and tearing into a lot of other projects. He does not want to spend evenings and weekends painting the garage or redecorating the bedroom or pruning the trees or going shopping or anything else.

It seems to Joe that his wife, Ginger, is dissatisfied a lot. She criticizes him. Even when she does not say anything it is not hard to tell that she is not very approving. Joe thinks that Ginger considers him lazy and sloppy because he is not interested in sprucing up the home and is not even very interested in his own appearance. From Joe's point of view, home has become a part of the world to be competed with and defended from. Home is not a sanctuary from the world for him. It is a projection of disagreeable demands which remind him too much of the business world he is trying to find relief from.

Joe has been talking a lot with a woman he sees at work. She understands the strains he is under and is totally sympathetic and approving. She does not see it as her function to correct or change Joe. She knows he is having a hard time both at work and at home. Because of her involvement in the business situation she is able to share more intelligently the kinds of stresses Joe experiences at work. She is neither vicious nor seductive. She is simply a decent, caring person whose natural sympathies are supportive to Joe. Joe finds himself wanting to be with her more, he suspects, than he should.

Another complicating factor in Joe's life is his kids. To him they seem noisy, ungrateful, and thoughtless. It is a hassle to get them to do simple things like make their beds and hang up their clothes. Their table manners are bad and they are disrespectful. He knows that they don't realize how hard he tries to take care of their needs. They waste food and electricity. They lose coats and tennis shoes. They have to be driven everywhere in the car. They complain about everything they are asked to do. They never cease to ask for money.

The car needs new tires and soon will have to have a brake job. The old roof will only last another year or two, and the price of shingles is out of reason. Conditions are getting worse so that the repairs Joe cannot afford now will be more expensive if he puts them off.

Joe has put on a few pounds. He is not as trim and athletic looking as he used to be. He wonders if he is getting old and what it will be like to be old. He is beginning to suspect that he will never enjoy the business and social success he had anticipated. He questions his intelligence and business ability. He is not as confident or aggressive as he used to be.

These and a thousand other factors are a part of the world Joe lives in. Whatever Christlikeness he is able to muster has to be in this context. Joe cannot function as a Christian separate from the world he lives in. He must function within that world. This is a part of what it means that the Word became flesh. Jesus was born into a real world, a complicated world, a frustrating world.

Ginger's World

The picture is not complete when we think of Joe's problems. He does not live in isolation but interacts with many other people. All of the components of his life are, to a lesser degree, components of all these other lives. The result is an inconceivably complex web of factors which affect all of these lives and ultimately all mankind. Of course, Joe's world has the most direct bearing on the life of his wife, Ginger.

Ginger is forty-one and is not as comfortable as she used to be about being a year older than Joe. When they married they laughed about this slight difference in age. Now that Ginger is less secure in her feeling of physical attractiveness her age is no laughing matter.

Ginger is twenty pounds overweight. She feels plain and unattractive. Her self-image is one of drabness. She is convinced that Joe sees her in this light too because he seems to take her so much for granted. The freshness, warmth, and excitement have disappeared from their love. Joe and Ginger share only mundane things like food, lodging, bills, chores, and responsibilities. No longer do they share a feeling of romance. Ginger feels that they never talk.

"How did your day go?"

"Fine. Yours?"

"Not bad. The repairman came to fix the washing machine."

"What would you like to do tonight?"

"It doesn't matter."

Ginger's world also is one in which the kids are growing up. They don't need her as much as they used to. They do things she does not approve. She doesn't know how much freedom to give and how much control to exert. She secretly fears that she has little control at all. All of her visions of the fruition of motherhood are swallowed up in the kids' search for independence. She wants to hold them close to comfort her insecurity. They want to cut the apron strings to experience adulthood.

At the same time the kids are pulling away, it seems to Ginger that Joe is pulling away also. He never appears to want to be with her. He is totally immersed in his problems and his work. More and more Joe has cut himself off from the things they used to do together. He does not even seem to have much interest in the house anymore. "It wouldn't take him long to paint the garage," Ginger reasons, "and that bedroom does need redecorating."

Ginger has her financial problems too. "Has anybody noticed grocery prices lately?" she wonders, "and the price of clothes is out of sight." She cleans and shops and sews and cooks and at last drops into her chair at dinner and what does she hear?

"Where's the butter?"

"Mother, you know I don't like beets."

"I'm sick of casseroles."

After dinner, Ginger may hopefully ask, "Would somebody please help me in the kitchen?" Then the chorus begins.

"I have a meeting at church."

"I have to study."

"I've already invited Sammy over."

"I've worked hard all day. It looks like you at least could keep the house and fix the meals."

Ginger has not been feeling well lately. She wonders whether there might be something seriously wrong or whether she is exaggerating the symptoms. It has been two years since she had a checkup. If she went to the doctor, would he take her seriously or would he treat her like a bored suburban hypochondriac?

These factors just give us a glimpse of all the questions, fears, and complicating forces that are involved in Ginger's world. Whatever ministry for God she has must be in this world. She can work at improving it, but she cannot choose another. This is another insight into what it means that Jesus came into the world. He came into a world inhabited by people who were interrelated in many ways at many levels. Often their relationships were frightening and destructive. The Word became flesh and lived in our world.

The Kids' World

The tensions crackle when the Sanders kids walk through their back door. Any inclination they had to be thoughtful and cheerful is quickly batted down.

"Where are your books? Your bed is not made. Don't forget to turn out the lights. Don't throw your coat down. Do your homework."

The kids have already had two or three pretty good chewing outs at school. They probably provoked some of them. Some seemed to come right out of the blue. Their teachers live in worlds as complex as those of their parents. Sometimes they ventilate their frustrations on students for reasons that have nothing at all to do with the students.

Debbie is upset because she is doing badly in math and she knows what a family scene report card time will bring. Jimmy was pushed down by a bully on his way home from school. The boy Debbie likes likes somebody else. Dad wants Jimmy to make the football team, but Jimmy doesn't like football. Jimmy has to try to decide whether it would be worse to go out for football or to have Dad think him a sissy.

Jimmy doesn't want a haircut. Mom wants Debbie to dress up, she prefers old jeans. Both kids feel that they don't have any money. They don't know where or how to get a job, and they feel that Dad thinks they are lazy. Somebody stole Jimmy's bicycle out of the garage. Both are secretly afraid they are not as smart as other kids. Debbie is afraid that she will never have a boyfriend.

These are just a handful of the complicating factors in

the lives of Debbie and Jimmy. They would really have their hands full if they did not have any problems relating to their mother and dad. This is their world. If they are going to be Christian it must be in this world. They cannot choose a simple uncomplicated arena in which to make Christian decisions. They have to make those decisions under the pressures and strains of the world they live in. That is why it is important to them that the Word became flesh and lived in their world.

The Melting Pot

We have looked at the Sanders family divided into compartments. Actually they do not live in compartments, but in a single world in which they, with all the complicated baggage of their lives, bump into all others who also carry all the assorted tangles of their own lives. This is the world. Jesus came into the world for us. He came into this complex frustrating world to show us what God is like in the context in which we must know Him and serve Him.

This is one of the reasons that many did not recognize Jesus. They were looking for something different. They expected a Savior who was more pious, more saintly, and more religious. It was not easy for the people who saw Jesus to understand that God could be in their world on that particular day.

It is not easy for us to understand that if we are to follow Christ at all it will have to be on a day like today and in a world like this one. We cannot wait until we get things straightened out. We cannot put it off until we find a model church. We cannot stall until our family becomes more understanding.

We tend to forget that the Lord's arena is the world. He came in the flesh. We trudge along waiting for another time and another place. He is with us and we do not recognize Him. While we watch the distant horizon for His entry, He is standing beside us.

4

Dream Come True

It is hard to imagine a story that would be more satisfying than one in which an old man had the dream of a lifetime fulfilled when he held a baby in his arms. Such is the story of Simeon and Jesus. While Luke is not explicit about Simeon's age, the account infers that he was in advanced years. Luke 2:26 says that this was to be fulfilled before his death. Verse 29 indicates that Simeon was then prepared to die when the promise had been fulfilled. The occasion of the aged Simeon holding the baby Jesus in his arms is a marvelous story.

The Promise Kept

This is the narrative of a gentle old man who had lived a lifetime in trusting anticipation of the fulfillment of God's

---

Scripture Resource: Luke 2:21-38

promise. Simeon was righteous and devout. He never stopped looking forward to the coming of the Messiah. We can imagine that on a number of occasions he must have been sick or discouraged, but he never seems to have lost his confidence in the Lord's promise.

The Holy Spirit had revealed to Simeon that he would see the Christ before he died. Simeon knew that such a promise was a dependable and secure one. What God has said will happen will happen. God's Word is truth in a very profound way. His very nature is truth. Whatever He says is a projection of that nature.

For God to say, "Let there be light," is for Him to create light. God's nature is so formative, so creative, that for Him to say a thing is to assure its truthfulness. What He says about the future is as certain as what He says about the present or past. He speaks of the future as certainly as though it had already happened.

When we say something that is true, it is because we are accurately reporting facts that exist independently from our statements. There is a possibility that when we speak there will be a discrepancy between what we say and the real state of things.

When God speaks, however, His world is so identical with truth as to cause it to happen. Facts do not exist independently from Him. There is no possibility of a gap between what He says and the way things are. Another way of saying "God's Word is truth" is "God's Word is reality." What God says is the way things really are.

Therefore when God makes a promise, you can bank on it as though it has already happened. Simeon knew where to place his trust. He knew that although dozens of generations of Israelite people had anticipated the coming of the Messiah in their lifetimes, that the Messiah actually would come in his lifetime. Previous generations hoped. They expected. Simeon believed. He knew.

Sometimes a promise of God is not kept in the way we expect. Simeon may have expected the Messiah to arrive on the scene in a more dramatic way. God does not promise to do things the way we expect, but what He promises will be done.

"I'd like to deposit three promises of God: two in savings and one in checking."

Sometimes a promise of God will not be kept at the time we expect. In fact, some people lost confidence in God's promise because the time in which they expected it to be fulfilled had passed. Abraham and Sarah expected to have a son at an earlier age than they did. Simeon may have expected to see the Christ at an earlier date. God does not promise to operate on our timetable, but He does promise to fulfill His Word.

Inspired by the Spirit, Simeon went into the temple at the right moment to see the baby Jesus. The Lord's promises are kept. They are kept in His time and in His way, but they are always kept.

In His Arms

Simeon took Jesus in his arms and blessed God. What a beautiful fulfillment of promise! This old man, whose eyes were dimmed with the passing years but whose trust was unabated, held in his arms the hope of Israel.

The fact that Simeon took Jesus in his arms reminds us about the nearness and the touchableness of God's promises. When God keeps His promise it is not in a remote or abstract way. It is in a personal and direct way. God is working out His will in the world we can see and touch. He has not given us a theory, but a person.

Another subtle lesson from this passage is the interrelatedness of youth and age. Here is an old man about to pass from the scene and a baby who just arrived on it. They are not separated into two different compartments of life. They fit together. Each has his appropriate role to play in the working out of the will of God on earth. The coming of the Christ was not in any way a threat to the life, work, purpose, or destiny of the old man. The existence of the man who loved and trusted God was not competitive with the baby who was the central expression of the will of God for man.

In much the same way we can see how those of various ages can work together to do the will of God on earth. Those who are old in years have a meaning and ministry that is vital to the completion of God's work. Their importance is in no way a threat to those who are younger. The young also have their distinctive role to fulfill to do the will of God. They can do it fully and exuberantly without encroaching on the identity or usefulness of the old. The grace of God is so great that it requires all men to reflect adequately all the varied aspects of it. We are not competitors with any others. There can never be too much love, too much mercy, too much forgiveness, or too much understanding. All of us can do the will of God to the fullest extent of our ability without getting in the way of or stepping on the toes of others.

This tender picture of the old man and the baby also reminds us of the gentleness of God's care. The man's deepest yearnings and needs were met in the most excellent way possible. In the same setting God was preparing

Mary and Joseph to better understand the work Jesus would be doing. In doing this, God provided for Jesus the kind of a home that it would be important for Him to grow up in. In an interlocking way God works through His people to meet the needs of one another.

As we consider the people who surround us, we are again impressed with the fact that God's care is more extensive than we can imagine. Even in our fondest dreams we would not dare to ask for the blessings that He has planned for us. As Simeon, apart from the revelation of the Holy Spirit, would not have expected to hold the Christ, so we will have blessings that, apart from God's Word, we could never expect.

It is important that we, like Simeon, continue to trust God for His blessings. This keeps our lives open to His working. He is never stingy with His gifts. Sometimes our trust is so small that we allow only the smaller of His blessings to enter.

Go in Peace

"Now I can die in peace because the purpose of my life has been fulfilled," Simeon said. How beautiful and how rare it is for a person to have such a clear sense of purpose that he can feel that his life is completed, not simply ended.

Many people do not know when their work is done because they do not know what they are supposed to be doing. They have never clearly resolved what they wish to do with their lives. They wander through life dabbling with this interest or that one but without a dominant theme or direction. They are like someone's description of an onion: all layers but no core.

It is understandable how this could happen. It's not easy to do the thinking and make the commitment necessary to a purposeful life. It means accepting some disciplines, paying some costs, and giving up some peripheral interests. Many people would like to find an easier way to purposeful living. There is no easier way. Neither is there a sense of completion where there is no sense of purpose.

A Sword-pierced Soul

Simeon told Mary, "A sword will pierce through your soul." He was warning her about the cost of love or the cost of being called by God. The two are one. Love is what God calls us to. Love is what God called Mary to. In her case the call was more intense because it would involve her in the focal point of God's plan for mankind.

Regardless of how glorious the honor of God's call, there can be no exemptions to the price of love. God himself paid it in the giving of Christ. Jesus paid it in His suffering and death. Mary paid it in the pain to a mother's heart when her son was abused and unjustly murdered. We pay it when we love. There is no way to be lovingly involved in another's life without being hurt when he hurts and sorrowful when he is away.

Those who seek love without pain seek an illusion. There is no love without pain. On the other hand, there is pain without love. There is the pain of loneliness, of selfishness, and of incompleteness, of realizing that we tend to want to love but not to be hurt.

Several years ago a friend of mine was widowed when his wife died suddenly of a brain tumor. This man was so dependent on his wife that he found it difficult to survive alone. He sought escape in his work and eventually in drugs. I urged him to develop new relationships, to come out of his shell, and to be with people. Tears would come in his eyes as he would try to explain to me the almost unbearable nature of his hurt. He could not stand to think of being so deeply hurt again. Therefore he was afraid to love.

This man knew something very true about the nature of love. He knew that he either had to accept the pain that goes with it or forego it completely. After a painful search my friend eventually became able to expose himself to the possibility of hurt again. He has since married, and now lives a loving and happy life. He is accepting the risk of loving.

Simeon was warning Mary that loving Jesus would bring pain and sorrow into her life. It is certainly worth much more than it costs to love Him, but no one should be deceived into thinking that Jesus can be loved cheaply. "A sword will pierce through your soul," could, to a lesser degree, also be said to all of us who love Jesus.

God's People Are One

The cast of characters in this narrative deserve notice. We have Simeon, the devout old gentleman who has waited long to see the Lord. We have Mary, the young Jewish mother who is caught up in a drama much larger than she is. Then there is Joseph, Mary's young and undoubtedly confused husband. In the latter verses we read of Anna, the aged prophetess who had for so long fasted and prayed.

At the center of them all is the baby Jesus. Men and women, old and young, all of them find their center in Jesus. So it is in our world today. The love of God transcends all barriers and gaps to create a genuine oneness between those of advanced years and those who are just starting the journey of life. One of the very encouraging things happening in our society is the increasing appreciative notice the young and old are taking of each other. They need each other. They need each other's love.

5

Perfect—at First, at Last

From the Beginning

The last part of Luke 2 tells the remarkable story of the growth of one whose starting point was perfection. Literally, from the beginning Jesus was divine. "In the beginning was the Word, and the Word was with God, and the Word was God.... And the Word became flesh and dwelt among us, full of grace and truth; we have beheld his glory, glory as of the only Son from the Father" (John 1:1, 14). How could one who started out as the divine Word grow from infancy to manhood? Even stranger, how could He grow spiritually?

Jesus did not give up His divinity in being born in order to gain it back later as He grew. He was as divine at His birth as He was later. The angel told Mary, "The Holy

---

Scripture Resource: Luke 2:39-52

Spirit will come upon you, and the power of the Most High will overshadow you; therefore the child to be born will be called holy, the Son of God" (Luke 1:35). The Lord's divinity and sonship were not attained through growth. They were His to begin with. They were never in doubt.

Yet Luke tells us that Jesus grew, not only in stature, but also in wisdom and in favor with God. How did He grow? Perhaps this can best be explained by looking at three occasions when He commented on His mission in the world.

When Jesus was twelve years old He went to Jerusalem with His parents. It was an annual practice of Mary and Joseph to be in Jerusalem for the Passover. They were a faithful and dutiful family. They took their religious duties seriously. It is significant that when God was selecting the people who would be responsible for the rearing of His own Son, He picked people like this. While the religion of God is not unduly restrictive or repressive, it is strengthened by regular spiritual disciplines.

In modern times we have seen a fascination with the spontaneous expression of religion which sometimes scorns structure or planning. This point of view places a great deal of emphasis on doing what one feels like doing at the moment. It implies that acts of worship or service done on a regular and planned basis are lacking in sincerity and spirit. This leads to an erratic type of religious life which swings wildly from ecstasy to depression.

While Mary and Joseph undoubtedly had moments of unusual exhilaration and moments of serious discouragement, they also had a stable and consistent program of spiritual activity which they followed carefully. This included going to Jerusalem every year to celebrate the Passover.

When the feast was over and Mary and Joseph started home, Jesus stayed behind. Supposing that Jesus was among relatives, Mary and Joseph did not notice His absence for a day. Then they returned to Jerusalem where they looked for their Son for three days before finding Him in the temple. Their very natural question was, "Son, why have you treated us so? Behold, your father and I have been looking for you anxiously" (Luke 2:48).

Jesus' answer records His first statement of His sense of mission, "Did you not know that I must be in my Father's house?" (Luke 2:49). Already Jesus had an understanding of the uniqueness of His ministry which His parents did not possess. He knew that His real reason for being in the world was to do God's will. Even at this point, Jesus knew that it was His to do whatever God wanted. However, being only twelve and having voluntarily accepted limitations in becoming human, He does not appear to have been fully aware of the implications of giving himself to the Father's will.

My Food Is to Obey the Father

After Jesus had begun His ministry, He made another statement about His purpose in life. He and His disciples were traveling through Samaria when Jesus became weary from the journey. He sat down to rest by a well while the disciples went into the city of Sychar to buy food. In their absence Jesus had the famous conversation with the Samaritan woman in which He taught her that God was not locked into any sectarian system but was the God of all people. Jesus told her that she would find God, not through an institutional connection, but by worshiping Him in spirit and truth (John 4:24).

When the disciples returned with food they urged the Lord to eat. They knew that He was tired and hungry and needed nourishment. His response was, "My food is to do the will of him who sent me, and to accomplish his work" (John 4:34).

Jesus' statement affirmed the same basic truth He had earlier declared when He said, "I must be in my Father's house." The difference between the two statements is this: now He was experiencing the fact that doing the Father's will was really more important to Him than sustaining physical life.

There is a great difference between understanding something academically and understanding something from experience. We all understand a great deal about courage, honesty, unselfishness, and humility if we are discussing these qualities. Yet when we get into a real life situation in which emotions color attitudes and costs become painful and real, it is a different matter. Jesus was absolutely sincere about giving His life to God when He was twelve, but He understood a lot more when He was thirty or so.

He Learned Obedience

It was the total giving of himself on the cross that enabled Jesus to understand fully what it meant to be God's man. When He came to the eve of this event, He had to wrestle again with that basic commitment which He had first expressed when He was twelve. He did this wrestling in Gethsemane. It was not that He had second thoughts about whether His life belonged to God. It was rather that He was having deepening thoughts about what it meant for His life to belong to God. Being God's man had led Him to the foot of the cross. Was there a way to be God's man and avoid this terrible and tragic pain and humiliation? In answer to this question Jesus prayed, "Not my will, but thine be done" (Luke 22:42).

Jesus was never disobedient to God, but He did not fully know what obedience was except in the cross. Therefore the author of Hebrews could say, "Although he was a Son, he learned obedience through what he suffered; and being made perfect he became the source of eternal salvation to all who obey him" (Hebrews 5:8, 9).

At last it could be said that He had been made perfect. It was not that He had ever been less than flawless. It was that now He had a depth of obedience that had increased until He fully knew what it was to be totally God's man. Jesus had been tempered in the fires of suffering until His will was as strong as steel and it belonged completely to God. He was able to be God's man in a way that a selfish, indulgent person could never be.

It is also notable that this obedience doesn't come with rank or position. The fact that Jesus was God's Son did not give Him automatic maturity in obedience. He gained that by obeying God in difficult and costly situations.

Your Identity

As Jesus had an early awareness of His identity and mission, so you can also have a clear commitment to God even when you are quite young. You were made by God. You were made in His image. You were made to relate to Him, belong to Him. You were made to be His child. As you realize this and give yourself to him, you become His.

You are as fully His from the first day of your new birth as you will be fifty or sixty years later. A one week-old oak tree is as certainly an oak tree as a one hundred year-old oak tree. The difference is that one has experienced more years, more storms, more droughts, and more growth than the other. When the younger one has lived for one hundred years it will have the same kind of deep roots, massive trunk, and strong branches that the older one has. When the younger one has lived all these years it will still not be any more an oak tree than it is already.

When you become a Christian, you belong fully and securely to Christ. If you live to be one hundred years old and grow spiritually during all of those years, you will not be more certainly a Christian then than you are at the beginning. Yet you will have deeper roots, greater understanding, stronger endurance, and more tender compassion than you have now. You will have learned obedience in a deeper and more mature way. It will be possible for you to be God's person then at a depth that is greater than you can now imagine. You will appreciate more fully the implications of doing the will of God.

This is how there can be perfect security in Christ and, at the same time, room for growth. In much the same way Jesus was God's unique Son from the beginning, and yet He was able to experience spiritual growth to the point of being able to give His life for others.

Your Goal

The goal of your spiritual development is not simply adequate church membership. You have that already when you begin the Christian walk. Your objective is the kind of spiritual maturity that enabled Christ to go to the cross. You are to try to develop, in the storms and trials of life, the quality of obedience that Christ demonstrated.

What qualities can I expect to develop in my life as I grow in the likeness of Christ? One important quality is integrity under pressure. Even when we are young we learn truthfulness in the sense that we should not tell lies. Beyond that our truthfulness must deepen until we can face death in preference to being dishonest about who we really are or what we really believe. This is the kind of integrity with which Jesus faced Pilate. Pilate was surprised that Jesus did not buckle under the threat of losing His life. Jesus was able to go calmly to the cross. To Him death was better than pretense.

Another is endurance. It takes deep roots that have weathered many storms to be able to persevere after a long series of setbacks and discouragements. Those who continue to pursue a true course in spite of disappointmont, ridicule, and persecution have reached a significant state of Christlike maturity.

Another is consistency. It is always easy to be Christian toward some people under some circumstances at some times. It is when we try to be Christian toward all people under all circumstances and at all times that we learn how strong Christian maturity needs to be. The problem comes when we have to be kind to someone we do not like, return good to someone who has done evil to us, and pray for one who has abused us. We are supposed to respond that way even when we are tired and discouraged. And we are expected to behave like that time after time instead of just once.

Another is initiative. It is easier to do what someone tells us to do than it is to assess the situation, determine what the Christian course is, and implement it on our own. "Nobody gave me anything to do," is the complaint of the immature Christian. "The world is full of people to love and serve," is the observation of the mature Christian.

Still another is magnanimity, largeness of spirit. When we are juvenile in Christ we are concerned with slights and jealousies. We are easily peeved. We pout and act in petty ways. As we grow up in Christ we begin to see the childishness of such behavior. We begin to understand that having good relationships with God and with people is far more important than any real or imagined hurt we may have experienced. We then begin to develop an expansive and humane spirit that is generously forgiving and joyously accepting. We get over the tendency to be harsh and judgmental. We become pure and clear reflections of the love of God for sinful men.

Perfect Yet Growing

From the very beginning Jesus was the perfect Son of God. Still He grew to manhood and eventually to the perfect and mature obedience to the will of God that expressed itself in the cross. There was now no expectation of the will of God that He had not fully obeyed. May we, in our lives, grow toward that exalted goal.

6

A Life's Work Launched

Strange and Wonderful

The next time you go into a card shop, look for my favorite card. On the front it says, "Ours is a strange and wonderful relationship . . ." The punch line inside reads, "You're strange, and I'm wonderful!"

John the Baptist was both strange and wonderful. He was strange because he was unconcerned about status. He did not appear to have any concern about what people thought of him. He had a job to do. He was pointing the way to Jesus. To him, it didn't matter much whether or not people were impressed with John.

John was a rugged and independent sort of a preacher. He had no use for political games or soft living. He preached in the wilderness. This was a desolate and

---

Scripture Resource: Mark 1:4-13

rough area. John didn't go to the centers of population where it would be easy for people to hear him. The people had to make a significant effort to hear what John had to say. His clothing was not the soft and refined clothing of the orators of the day, but was the tough and durable garb of the outdoorsman. His food was the simplest and most natural fare.

John was strange in that in him one could see both austerity and love. We get the feeling that he was a gruff lover of people. He had no patience with sham and hypocrisy, but he had a passionate concern to see lives centered in God. This concern glistened in the earnestness of his preaching. John had a strange combination of defiance of the society of his day and a care for the individuals who made up that society.

This strange man was wonderful in the most basic meaning of that term. He inspired wonder and awe. Both his admirers and his enemies had a respect that approached fear. He saw things clearly and spoke candidly. Many feared he would observe some hidden deceit in their lives and expose it in the sight of all. They knew John would never be dissuaded by flattery, pressure, or bribery.

John was awe-inspiring because of his unchallengeable honesty. He was without pretense. He did not manipulate people to get them to do what he thought they ought to do. He told them frankly what their duty to God was and allowed them to respond in whatever way they would.

John was awe-inspiring because of his unassuming elevation of Christ. Most men's actions can be readily explained on the basis of self-interest. Many businessmen won't enter into a contract until they see what is in it for the other person. They figure that everybody is out for himself. If they cannot see how the other person expects to profit, they assume there is something about the contract that they do not understand. That is why advertisers offer the customer a reason why they sell merchandise at such a low price. "We are overstocked ... We have lost our lease ...The merchandise has slight defects ... This was purchased at a special price ..." The merchant figures that we won't believe him unless he explains how his self-interest is served by selling us merchandise at such a low price.

John the Baptist did not do that. He simply said, "After me comes he who is mightier than I, the thong of whose sandals I am not worthy to stoop down and untie" (Mark 1:7). In effect John was saying, "I have no hidden motive. I am not preaching Jesus in order to be benefited myself. I preach Him because He is the Lamb of God, and you should worship Him."

Such a direct approach was a brilliant preparation for the coming of Christ. John, in the very way he presented Christ, made it clear that the Messiah was to be different from what was generally expected.

Originals

While John's honesty and courage were much like Christ, John was in many ways very different from the Lord. Both were originals. Both were powerfully used by God. Either would have been weakened by trying to copy the other.

It is important for you to note that devotion to Jesus did not prevent John from being a truly distinct personality. For you, too, are an original. You are endowed by God with a unique ability to reflect some facet of His grace to your world. It is important for you to be true to who you are. In doing so you will be true to the God who made you.

A friend of mine is presently fascinated with the paintings of a certain modern artist. The artist's paintings are so popular that well-made copies are selling fast. Although printing techniques are now so excellent that the copies are extraordinarily well-done, they are still worth only a small fraction of the value of an original. Where an original might sell for $8000, a print could be bought for $35. Even the smallest and crudest original would be worth many times more than the most excellent print.

The same principle applies to your finding your unique place in the service of God. Copies are worth little. Originals are worth much. Even the least talented person who is an authentic original will be far more powerful as an influence for God than the most polished copy.

Do not despair that you are not like another. Instead rejoice in your individuality. Discover your strengths and abilities. Recognize that the full and imaginative use of them in the service of God will have a far greater impact than even an excellent facsimile of a multi-talented idol of yours.

A Decisive Starting Point

Jesus had been the Son of God all His life. He had been conscious of obeying God and serving God since childhood. His baptism was not so much a change of direction as a decisive point of commitment to His life's work. This is where He began His public ministry.

Our lives need a point like that. Some of us were reared in Christian homes. We have always been believers. We have always loved God. Some of our earliest teachings were that God made the world, the flowers, the food, our parents, and us. We learned to thank Him and pray to Him long before we were capable of any critical philosophical thinking about whether or not we believed in God. God has always been a part of our lives. It is as natural to believe as to breathe or walk or talk.

Not only have we always believed but we have always had a desire to please Him and obey Him. Even so, if our lives are to have the real thrust of a sense of mission, we have to experience a point of decisive commitment. One does not just drift into that kind of purposeful life. He drives into it deliberately, and with determination.

Others of us have had real periods of rebellion and disobedience. We strongly needed a decisive turning point. Our lives were strongly out of character for a good relationship with God. We needed to bring forth fruits worthy of repentance.

In either case Christianity is not a process of absorption. It is the result of a decision of faith, acted upon with resolution. If this was important to Christ, it is vastly more so to us. Rather than being spiritual drifters we ought to make a strong, determined decision to use our lives in a specific way to serve God.

An Abrupt Awakening

As soon as Jesus came up from the water of baptism and God affirmed His sonship, the Spirit drove Him into the wilderness. There He fasted for forty days and was tempted by Satan.

At first this seems to be a strange sequence of events. The public confirmation of God's approval is followed instantly by a soul-wrenching struggle with hunger and temptation. More reflection, however, helps us to understand the relationship between these two.

The first occurrence, confirmation of God's acceptance, is the soil in which all Christian living is rooted. The second, the call to obey God at great cost, is the inevitable result of belonging to God. With God secure acceptance and great expectation go together. They are the two facets of love. Belonging securely to God is not an escape from discipleship but a call to it. God's demand for disciplined discipleship is not a denial of security but an expression of it.

This is not only true of our relationship with God but also of all other relationships. A relationship where one only gives and the other only takes is not based on authentic love. It cannot survive. This is not because of the impoverishment of the giver but because of the erosion of the taker. He cannot tolerate the rejection implicit in continually having nothing expected of him. Such an attitude says to him, "You are nothing. You are a nobody. You have nothing worthwhile to give. You are a zero." When we really love somebody, we expect him to be a full partner in the relationship.

This is true of a youth's relationship to his parents. He may say or imply, "You don't love me or you would not expect that of me." He is wrong to think that true love makes no expectations. God loved His Son and He expected Him to go to the cross.

Parents should expect their sons and daughters to be people of honesty, courage, and strength. Without love a parent might be able to tolerate a backbone of jelly. If he didn't care, the parent might accept the fact that a son or daughter lies, cheats, bullies the weak, and collapses under pressure. This will not happen if the parent loves his child. It will not happen if the youth is seen as a person of worth and significance. The parent who loves his offspring will want him to be a person of principle, a person who can be trusted, a person of inner substance.

The wilderness of struggle and temptation is the inevitable next step when one accepts Christ. Expectation follows acceptance because they are both a part of love. Christ never called followers on the basis of the ease of discipleship. He always assured people of God's love and called them to a life of devotion and obedience.

Launching Your Life's Work

This vital experience in the life of Christ gives us some insight into a formative decision that we must make about our own lives. That is the decision in regard to vocation. How are we going to spend our lives? How will we earn our living? In what role will we spend the major part of our working time? These and related questions puzzle the minds of many of our young people.

A generation or two ago the decision was far less complex than it is now. There were fewer vocations to choose from. There was less change in the nature of a vocation during a lifetime. Perhaps one's vocational choice was even made for him by his parents or his station in life. The question of how to make a living was more prominent and the consideration of what is meaningful work was less important.

What guidelines can we gather from looking at the way in which Christ began His ministry? First, we should find a vocation that is truly a way of expressing Christian concerns. We should be very aware of the fact that every follower of Christ has a ministry all his own. The plumber, mechanic, teacher, or lawyer should seek opportunities to be an expression of the love of God to the world he lives in.

Second, we should recognize the need to be decisive. Making a big decision requires a great deal of courage. It is sometimes easier to drift aimlessly along hoping that something interesting will turn up. As Christ had an identity and mission to fulfill in His life, you have one in yours.

Third, we must remember that discipleship is demanding. Our choice of a lifetime work should not be made on the basis of that which can be done with little effort. It should be on the basis of where the greatest amount of good can be done.

When we have considered prayerfully and conscientiously these factors and made a decision, we can begin our career with confidence that God will see us through.

7

The Waiting Is Over

"George McCrocklin had a heart attack!" The news was abrupt and unwelcome. George had always been the very picture of robust good health. He was just in his early fifties. I would not have been surprised to pick up the phone and hear George's voice rushing to tell me of some new project or idea. I always thought of him in terms of activity, not sickness.

Now he was stricken down. He was seriously ill. The arteries supplying his heart were severely congested. His very life hung precariously in the balance.

Then came the surgery. It involved delicately giving anesthesia to a patient whose heart was already injured and struggling with a short blood supply. It meant taking out clogged sections of arteries and replacing them

---

Scripture Resource: Luke 4:14-24

with other tubing. Skill, timing, and teamwork had to be brought together in a disciplined arena. During the whole time George's fragile hold on life had to be protected.

In the waiting room another drama was unfolding. George's wife, Bonnie, wrung her hands anxiously during the seemingly unending hours. A single statement at any time could have announced, "It's over, he's gone." Bonnie, surrounded by her three daughters and other relatives and friends, had never felt so alone. Every waiting hour was torture. The fear and shock were almost unbearable.

At last the door, almost worn by the the eyes that had been glued to it, opened. George's surgeon appeared. The wait was over. "The news is good," he said.

The Wait Is Over

This is what Jesus was saying in Luke 4:21, "Today this scripture has been fulfilled in your hearing." The wait was over. The news was good. Since his expulsion from Eden man had walked a troubled and difficult path. Pain, sorrow, and hard work in unproductive soil had marked his existence. Man had been scarred by war, oppressed by bondage, and stifled by prison. He had been afflicted by disease and deprived by poverty.

For centuries, the Jewish people had looked forward to the coming of One who would bring relief, salvation, and hope. Isaiah had described him as the one who would bring "good news to the poor, release to the captives, recovering of sight to the blind, and liberty to the oppressed" (Isaiah 61:1 as quoted in Luke 4:18).

Yet generation after generation passed. Life was hard and discouraging. In many ways it got worse. Could they continue to believe in the coming of the Messiah, the one chosen of God to bring good news? Could they sustain hope?

It must have been something like watching that door in the hospital waiting room. The waiting, however, involved not hours, but lifetimes. Thousands had died while waiting. There was no certainty that other lifetimes would not pass before the promised Messiah would come. Undoubtedly many questioned whether He would ever come at all.

It would be impossible to exaggerate the profound significance of what Jesus said: "The wait is over. The news is good."

Waiting for What?

They were waiting for the one who, as Isaiah said, would bind up the brokenhearted. People had been subject to much condemnation and rejection and not much healing.

It seems that there is always a long line of people who are ready to tell you how wrong you are and how terrible life is. In fact, most of us are pretty good about doing that to ourselves. My observation has been that most, if not all, people have inadequate self-esteem at least part of the time. Sometimes a person's first reaction to this thought is, "I know some people who are so conceited they could never have a self-esteem problem." Some certainly give that impression. On knowing them better one often finds that apparent egotism is the defense erected to keep others from knowing how insecure and afraid a person is. The more he fears that others will learn of his inadequacy, the more aggressively he will maintain his mask of adequacy.

When we try to think of examples of people who do not have a self-esteem problem, we inevitably think of others. All of us seem to take for granted that we have such a problem. We just suppose that others do not. That is because we are aware of our own masks and sometimes are not aware that others are wearing masks too. Kahlil Gibran once said, "If we confessed our sins one to another we should laugh at one another for our lack of originality."

We secretly think we are not as smart as others, not as personable as others, not as skillful as others, or not as moral as others. We suppose that our secret sins are more shameful than those of others and that our capacity for spirituality is not as great as others. It may even be that compulsive religious activity has become a part of our mask. We wear it to keep others from suspecting that we are as bad as we secretly believe we are. Our tendency to be very critical of others is often an attempt to prevent them from observing our frailties. We assume that the best defense is a good offense. We believe that if another is trying to defend his life against our accusations, he will be diverted from making accusations about us.

We may defend ourselves to others, but we privately often judge ourselves harshly. We don't need a prosecuting attorney to convict us of our wrong. We already know it and feel judged by it. Our need is for a spiritual physician to bind up our broken hearts. We need healing, not rejection.

This is what the Jews were waiting for. They did not have a clear idea of what the Messiah would be like, but they did identify their welfare with the coming of the Messiah. Jesus said, "Today this scripture has been fulfilled in your hearing."

Surprised by Grace

When the people heard this, "they were surprised that words of such grace should fall from his lips" (Luke 4:22 NEB). It is hard to know what they were expecting. Perhaps they had been harangued so much with harsh judgment and condemnation that they were not expecting anything else. At any rate they were surprised that the long awaited Messiah would be gentle, kind, merciful, and forgiving.

Sometimes people today still find it surprising to learn that Jesus came to heal broken lives, not to condemn them. He always had a preference for being with those whom others rejected. He did not come to hang around with the good, but to minister to those who needed Him. He said it is the sick person who needs a doctor, not a well one. He urged people to learn the meaning of mercy.

It is a pleasant surprise to learn that Jesus did not come to condemn us but to help us. We do not have to hide from Him our hurts and shames. That would be like trying to keep fever a secret from your doctor. He needs to know so he can help you. A doctor does not get mad at you because you are sick. Neither does Jesus get mad at you because you are struggling with temptation. That is why Jesus came. If you were able to win the battle without His help, you would not need Him.

One reason we wear masks is because we fear that if others knew us as we really are, they would reject us. What a great blessing it is that Jesus knows us as we really are and still loves us and accepts us. Such remarkable good news helps explain why we are still surprised that words of such grace would come from His lips.

But What About . . . ?

Some fear that if we stopped condemning people and start accepting them lovingly, the moral structure of society might collapse. They somehow see their moral judgments to be essential to the preservation of decency and order in the world. What nonsense! The ethical structure of the universe is an expression of the nature of God himself. It will never collapse as long as God is who He is. It is not upheld by our feeble proclamations. It will not fall when we stop condemning people who violate it.

Instead of spending our time condemning the victims of sin, let us spend our time loving them and helping them. The condemning power is in the sin itself. We do not need to reinforce that. Let us rather reaffirm the good news: Christ came to bind up the brokenhearted.

This does not mean that we are ignoring the significance of sin. Sin is not made less sinful by grace. Wrong is not made right. Cancer is not made less harmful by a good surgeon. Yet a good surgeon may help one escape the harmfulness of cancer. With the good news of Christ, one may help many others escape the condemnation of sin.

What Is That to Me?

"If Christ came as good news to oppressed men, what does that mean to my personal life? How is He good news to me? What gracious message does He have for the tangles of guilt and fear that I experience?" These are questions that many of us might want to ask.

The answer is very encouraging. It says that though I feel insecure and afraid of being lost because of my sinfulness, Christ has good news for me. This is not because God does not take my sinfulness seriously. This is not because I have succeeded in overcoming my bad habits and sinful practices. It is not because I have been such a model Christian that I have found my own victory over sin.

It is rather that God takes my sin more seriously even than I do. He knows more about its heartache, its shame, its morale-destroying character, and its relationship-breaking nature than I do. He hates it. He sees it as a damnable infection that projects wanton destruction on His own beloved child.

The cross is the eternal answer to those who think that a gracious message underestimates the enormity of sin. The blood of Christ is the answer to those who question whether the gospel gives adequate emphasis to godly living. No other message has ever treated sin more seriously than the gospel. None has ever been less inclined to sweep it under a rug or ignore it in hope that it would go away. Christ represents an encounter with sin, not a whitewash job. He brings victory, not evasion. His good news is not based on weakness but strength.

8

Called to Discipleship

The narrative in Luke 5:1-11 is a clear lesson on the nature of discipleship. Simon, along with the other fishermen, had worked all night and had caught nothing. Weary with toil and discouragement, they had made their way to shore and were washing their nets. Their work was hard enough when they were successful. Scrubbing nets after a long night of failure was even worse.

Jesus told Simon, "Put out into the deep and let down your nets for a catch." Simon blurted out his objection, "Master, we toiled all night and took nothing!" Then, thinking better, he added, "But at your word I will let down the nets." When he did so the nets were filled to the breaking point.

Simon was a tempestuous but likable man. He had

Scripture Resource: Luke 5:1-11

probably worked harder than anyone else during the long night. He was probably more tired and more frustrated. He was the most outspoken in his reaction to Jesus' directive to let down the nets again. He was also quickest to change his mind when he realized his mistake.

When the big catch of fish was brought up Simon stammered, "Depart from me, for I am a sinful man, O Lord." This very alive, responsive, turbulent man had run the gamut of emotions in just a brief period of time.

It was then that Jesus gave His real charge, "Do not be afraid; henceforth you will be catching men." They were so deeply impressed they left everything and followed Him. Here we learn something about the nature of discipleship. It means to follow another.

Suppose a friend asked you to go with him without specifying where he was going. Suppose you responded with confidence in your friend by going with him without further inquiry. The two of you might go out the door, down the street, through a park, into a store, and finally back to your starting point. That would demonstrate something of what it means to be a disciple. Note what happens.

Not Arriving but Following

Discipleship centers not on a place but on a person. The essence of it is not going to church, but following Jesus. When you went with your friend, you were not guided by a certain destination or route but by a certain person. When Jesus called the fishermen, He didn't call them to go to a certain location, but to follow Him. As far as we know, they had no idea what following would involve. They didn't know where it would take them or what they would be doing. They had no advance warning of the risks or costs of following.

Because the fishermen decided to follow Christ they had many difficult and painful experiences. Some were imprisoned, some were beaten, and many were killed. They spent their lives without the benefit of regular paychecks. Much of the time, there was no assurance of the next meal or a place to spend the night. They had to have an enormous amount of trust in Him to follow under such circumstances.

Today accepting the call to be a disciple of Jesus is not a matter of being at the right place or having your name on the right roll, but a matter of responding to every person and every situation as a follower of Jesus would respond.

Most of us have a strong inclination to build nests, comfortable sanctuaries where we are protected from the expectation to do the Christlike thing regardless of pain or cost. We like steady jobs and comfortable houses and best friends, and even predictable church relationships. We like to look for security in circumstances.

Discipleship will not allow it. It says your security is in following Jesus. It goes with you. Wherever He leads you are secure. He does not call you to accept a position or to occupy an office, but to follow Him.

His is a dynamic, not a static invitation. It is not meeting certain specifications but is signing a blank check for your life.

Not a Position but a Relationship

Discipleship is not just being able to answer religious questions correctly. It is not demonstrated by being doctrinally sound on all positions. It is being related to God in Christ.

Some young friends of mine, Lynn and Sandy Calhoun, have a son named Matt. Matt's security is not in his accomplishments but in his relationship to his mother and daddy. Suppose, after Matt is nearly grown, another boy comes up to Lynn and Sandy and says, "I want to take Matt's place. I am smarter than he is. Not only that but my behavior is a lot better than his." Lynn and Sandy would most certainly respond, "But Matt is our son."

As a matter of fact Matt is a very bright and sociable lad. It does not appear that he will have any trouble making an excellent performance record in school and in all other activities. Even then, however, his security will not be in his achievement, but in his relationship.

In the same way, no one can ever usurp the security of your relationship to the Lord on the basis of better achievements. Another may sing better, preach better, pray better, and know more Scripture. He may do more good works and give more money. Should he ever attempt to take your place with God because he has outperformed you, God would say, "But this one is my son," or "This one is my daughter."

This also reminds us that even if our achievements are outstanding we should not trust in them, but we should trust in Christ. Though you might be a golden tongued orator in the pulpit or an angel of mercy to the poor, your deepest spiritual security is in the fact that God has claimed you as His own. You are His.

Not a Fortress, but a Pilgrimage

Discipleship is not a fortress to be defended but a pilgrimage to be traveled. It is not a shrine around which admirers gather, but a journey which followers take. Early in this chapter we talked about you going on a walk with a friend. On such a walk you couldn't protect yourself by building a wall around you. Your movements would range too far for that. Your primary protection would be in your relationship with your friend.

When Jesus called the fishermen to follow Him, He did not promise them secure circumstances. He promised to be with them. Following Jesus never involves stopping to build a refuge.

The Christian life is like a river that maintains its purity by its movement. When water has no movement it becomes stagnant. It becomes a breeding ground for all sorts of corruption. The same is true of a life. The life that is not actively following Christ will become a breeding ground for self-centeredness, indulgence, self-pity, and other qualities that destroy spirituality.

In 2 Corinthians 5 Paul describes the body as a tent. It is a temporary residence, but not one in which we should try to put down roots. Our roots are in Heaven and we long to be there. Until then we, as Christians, are not interested in a permanent dwelling. We are interested in staying mobile and traveling light. The world is not our home. Our securities are not here. We are pilgrims and sojourners intent on making the journey with Christ.

Hebrews 11:8-10 describes Abraham as a man who was willing to leave his earthly home and go into a foreign land. He was willing to go from living in a fine house to living in tents. He was willing to change from secure citizenship to becoming a transient in an alien land. It is important to notice that Abraham followed God's instructions without knowing where they would lead him.

The reason Abraham was able to make such a giant step of faith is that he was seeking "the city which has foundations, whose builder and maker is God" (Hebrews 11:10). He did not trust in the security of his physical arrangements. His security was in God. Therefore he was secure when he went where God wanted him to go.

The admonition of Hebrews 12:1 is, "Let us throw off everything that hinders and the sin which so easily entangles, and let us run with perseverance the race marked out for us" (NIV). Let us not be burdened down with earthly accommodations. Let us not try to build a place of security on earth. Let us find our security in Christ. We will then enjoy the exhilarating freedom and mobility that come to the one who has internal rather than external security.

Not to Be Kept but to Be Given

Discipleship is not a self-satisfying treasure to be kept,

but a self-forgetting love to be given. Jesus did not call the fishermen to get something. He called them to become fishers of men. You are not called for what you will receive but for what you can give.

It is surprising how many people today complain that they have had no conversion experience. This is often because there has been no real conversion. They have not begun to love their enemies. They do not turn the other cheek. They have not gone the second mile. They do not rejoice in persecution. They have not found ways to lay down their lives for Jesus' sake. They are still as self-centered as ever. They see in Jesus a hope of satisfying desires that they have not been able to satisfy otherwise. They view Christianity as an opportunity to get blessings.

Rather than becoming disciples of Christ they snuggle further down into a nest of self-centeredness. Their religion is just another expression of their self-indulgent lives. They are certainly not following the life of Christ.

He who follows Christ learns to lose himself in the care of others. Instead of worrying about getting blessings, he is worrying about helping the poor, ministering to the sick, lifting up the fainthearted, and bringing mercy to the sinful.

It is not surprising that blessings come into such a life. They come in great abundance. The person who receives them will be surprised, perhaps overwhelmed at the blessings he receives. He will consider himself unworthy of the greatness of his blessings. He will increase his efforts to do good for others, and blessings will continue to be his. He may not ever really understand what is happening in his life because he is not expecting to get something. He finds his joy in giving.

In this he is like his Lord. He is following the Christ who did not worry about food or clothing for himself but only about helping others. He is following the Christ who was able to so forget His own welfare in love for others that

He could die on their behalf. He is learning that life is found by losing it and lost by trying to keep it.

What Do Disciples Do?

They do whatever is needed to express love and give service. Discipleship is never the same from day to day. Even the Samaritan who got down into the ditch to help a fellowman would not find the call the same every day. The important thing is to hear the calls that come to you and respond to them in the spirit of Christ. You never know where you will be led if you are sensitive and vulnerable to the calls to discipleship that come to you. Do what following Him would call you to do. That makes every day an exciting day.

9

Impostor Exposed

The Bible takes evil very seriously. It does not slough it off as if it were of no power or consequence. Neither is it defeated by evil. It affirms that God has won great victory over evil and that He is the indisputable sovereign of the universe. This means that when we grapple with temptation and sin we can know that it is not a mock battle. It also means that we can, in Christ, know that the ultimate battle has already been won and we need have no fear of losing our personal battle. On the one hand we are cautioned to make the battle, on the other hand we are assured that we will win it.

The Power of Darkness

It often seems that evil is particularly rampant in our

Scripture Resource: Mark 1:21-34

day. Some time ago I was reading about a church of Satan in San Francisco which has offshoot grottos in many cities and whose members number into the hundreds of thousands. Some groups participate in what they call black masses in which they employ every desecration of Christianity that is imaginable. It was reported that in Hollywood a church of Satan used as an altar a glass tank filled with formaldehyde and containing the body of a dead baby.

Even without these bizarre atrocities, we would not have much trouble documenting the fact that there is a lot of evil abroad in the land. Since Adam and Eve succumbed to the temptations of the devil in the Garden of Eden, men have done that which would seem unexplainable except for the existence of a power which seeks to propel us toward wrong.

Cain, out of jealousy, murdered his brother and then lied to God in an attempt to disclaim responsibility for the sin. Evil multiplied until the population of the earth had to be destroyed in the days of Noah. Even while Moses was on Mount Sinai receiving from God the Ten Commandments, the children of Israel lapsed into the worship of a false god.

So strong was the power of evil in those days that the sternest of laws had to be enacted for the preservation of society. If a man put out another's eye, society would put out his eye. If he broke out another's tooth, society would break out his tooth. Relatives were permitted, and even expected, to kill one who killed their relative. People were stoned to death for such things as adultery. It was, in many ways, a raw and rugged society that treated evil as a cancer that would destroy society. Society's response to sin was ruthless and decisive.

While we wouldn't want to go back to that system, we need to learn from those people that the power of sin is not a laughing matter. Sin has brought us death, sorrow, pain, degradation, and defeat.

The power of evil subjected Jesus to a physical and spiritual assault unparalleled in history. The pain, the despair, the anguish of isolation, and the spiritual burden of sin combined to make His battle unique. Satan understood the ultimate nature of his battle with Christ. Satan therefore unleashed every weapon in his arsenal. Physically, psychologically, and spiritually Satan used every device that he could hope would buckle Christ. Nowhere is the reality of the power of darkness more clearly exposed than in the crucifixion of Christ. Anyone who would question whether his own battle with sin is a sham battle finds his best answer here.

Since the crucifixion of Christ, evil in the world has continued to convince us that the power of darkness is real. Streaks of viciousness still bear witness to the fact that man is often more influenced by evil than by good. Our world is a world of war, oppression, racism, and crime. While we don't have many Hitlers who are responsible for the death of six million of their fellowmen, neither do we have many Albert Schweitzers.

Even in our own lives we have experienced enough of the power of darkness to identify with Paul's complaint, "I do not do the good I want, but the evil I do not want is what I do . . . when I want to do right, evil lies close at hand" (Romans 7:19). From every perspective it is all too painfully apparent that the power of darkness is real.

The Sovereignty of Christ

If the reality of the power of darkness were the whole story, it would be a bleak and discouraging picture. The power of darkness is real, but the power of Christ is stronger. This is emphasized throughout the New Testament. It is illustrated in the narrative of Mark 1:21-34. Jesus had power over even the unclean spirit that possessed the man in this text. The bystanders were amazed at the authority with which the Lord commanded such a demon. And this was not the only case in which Jesus displayed His power to cast out demons.

Whether or not one believes that personal demons can inhabit people today in the same sense this man was possessed, it is important to know that Jesus has the same power to conquer evil and free men that He had then. Christ demonstrated in this passage that men are no longer pawns in the power of evil. The stranglehold has been broken. The victory has been won. Our release has been secured.

Christ is without peer. No demon can equal Him. He excels them as the Creator excels the creature. He has power over all other powers both visible and invisible. No expression of the power of darkness can successfully challenge Him. In all things He is supreme. He does not share sovereignty. This is not a battle between powers of equal force, one evil and one good. It is rather a situation in which the one indisputable sovereign Lord Jesus Christ is challenged by a relatively weak and totally hopeless impostor who wrongly claims to be a world sovereign.

I have one friend who says, "The devil is not a power but a pest." That is probably overstating the case a bit but it does remind us that compared to Christ, the power of Satan has been shown to be ineffective.

Unfortunately it seems that some who are most impressed with Satan's fraudulent claim to absolute power are church members. We, of all people, ought to know that Christ is the sovereign Lord of all powers, both visible and invisible, both evil and good. Because of Jesus, we can refute the kingdom of darkness with its pompous appeal for the allegiance of men.

The Promise

If Jesus Christ is the undisputed sovereign of the world, what promise does that hold for us? First it promises wholeness. We do not have to go through life crippled and defeated. He is able to deal with whatever troubles we have and able to provide whatever resources we need. We don't have to fear that somewhere down the road we may meet a force that is too destructive for us to survive. There is no force that is so destructive that we will not be safe in Christ.

When we are anxious about emotional struggles, we can know that Christ is big enough to give us the strength that we need. The Christ who went through Gethsemane and to the cross knows what it is to be badgered from all sides and to have pressure that seems overwhelming. He has proved His ability to conquer and will make those who are in Him conquerors with Him.

When we feel defeated by temptations and sins that seem irresistible, we can know that Christ is Lord and He will give us the victory. This is no facile promise that relieves us of the need to make a spiritual struggle. Neither does it promise that temptations will go mysteriously away without effort on our part. Although the temptations are real and the battle will be hard, Christ has promised the victory. Even as a child learning to walk faces some stumbling and falling, so a young Christian learning to live like Christ will face some stumbling and falling. As the child's falls are not defeating to his ultimate purpose, neither are the Christian's falls defeating to his ultimate purpose. Christ will see us through even the most difficult and extended problem.

When we feel at the mercy of social pressure to do that which we believe wrong, we need to know that Christ is stronger than the social pressure. He was able to look the world in the eye, challenge its values, maintain His integrity, and conquer. He will enable us to conquer also.

Some feel helpless in the face of drugs or alcohol. They need also to experience the victory which is in Christ. Christ claimed control over our lives. He is not willing to relinquish control to a slave-master like addiction. We don't need to allow an uncontrolled appetite to dominate our lives. We can be free under Christ to make our own decisions and direct our own lives.

One of the things that His first-century audience found so refreshing about Christ is that He spoke in clear, understandable terms. He did not hedge. He did not waver. He did not say one thing to one person and another thing to others. He was not worried about the political effects of His plainspokenness.

Christ promises you the same kind of freedom. You can have the freedom to speak in clear and unambiguous terms. You don't need to be unnecessarily hostile, but you need not avoid saying what you believe. Because of your candor and honesty with all people, you will not be afraid that what you say on one occasion will come back to you on another. The remarkable kind of freedom that was impressive in the life of Christ is still impressive today.

Those who speak half-truths, those who conceal truths, those who deceive with flatteries, those who speak only that which is politically expedient, and those who speak to protect their own vested interests always speak weakly and guardedly. Only those who speak forthrightly can do so with confidence and authority. Because Jesus had no vested interest He was trying to protect, He could speak with unusual power and conviction.

Hurting and Healing

Tucked into this passage in Mark 1 is the story of the healing of Simon's mother-in-law. Before we leave the passage we should take note of that account. Here is a woman who is identified only by her relationship with Simon, that is, Peter. We do not even know the woman's name. What we do know is that she was suffering from an illness. This touched the Lord. "He came and took her by the hand and lifted her up, and the fever left her."

Jesus noticed people's hurts. He cared about them. He relieved them. Sometimes in your own life it will be very important to you to know that Jesus feels your hurts, cares about them, and will give you relief from them.

Sometimes in life it seems like we have to go for a long time without finding anyone who really understands or cares about the things that cause us pain. To feel that no one really cares is a very draining feeling. To know that there is One who is sensitively caring for our needs can bring us through many a dark hour.

Our Lord

All through this chapter we have been trying to say in a variety of ways that Jesus is the Lord of our lives. He is fully able and eager to respond to all of the needs that we have. No power, not even that of the devil himself, can keep Jesus from supplying our need and guaranteeing our victory. He is our Lord!

10

Authentic Power

Two incidents in Luke 7:11-23 emphasize how genuine the Lord is. In a world where we see so much phoniness, authenticity is especially striking. The first incident is the raising from the dead the widow's son. Jesus faced an inevitable and otherwise irreversible enemy of man. Others might fight valiantly to prevent death. It was unheard of for a person to challenge death itself. Jesus faced it squarely. He spoke and the dead man returned to life.

The second incident is the demonstration of good works intended to show John the Baptist that Jesus actually was the Christ. In both cases Jesus demonstrated His deep and unconquerable power.

Scripture Resource: Luke 7:11-23

He Cares

In the first occasion we note that Jesus had an uncommon amount of concern for the woman who lost her son. A young man had died. Jesus realized the significance. He did not offer platitudes. He did not shrug off death. He did not give an easy answer.

I read about a high school boy who was seriously injured in a car accident. The doctor told him that he would not be likely ever to play basketball or baseball again. This was especially painful to him because he was an excellent athlete. He expected to make all state in basketball and was hoping to finance a college education with athletic scholarships. The first afternoon he was able to have visitors a group of his school friends came in. They made a number of attempts to give comfort and reassurance. "I'm thankful you weren't killed." "It could have been worse." "I wish it hadn't happened."

Later a good friend asked the boy what words had given him the greatest amount of comfort. He said, "When Jerry was here he only said two words to me. He said, 'That's tough.' I felt like he understood my pain and cared about me. That meant more than any pretty speech he could have made."

A friend of mine lost his father a few years ago. He told me about the grief that his mother went through. The death broke up a marriage that had been unusually close for a period of fifty-two years. As friends gathered round to console the widow one said, "I know just how you feel." The widow rose up in indignation. "I'm sorry, but you don't," she replied. "I have lived with him for fifty-two years. Almost never did we even spend a night apart. His job was so that he could usually come home for lunch. When I went to the store he went with me. We have been as one for more than half a century and no one else could possibly know how I feel in losing him."

That woman was right. Our attempts to give easy generalizations in answer to death are offensive to those who are hurting with a unique pain. Jesus did not try to do that. He did not give any easy answers. He simply had compassion. He sensed the enormity of her loss and hurt.

The man who died was the only son of his mother. Jesus realized that there is a distinct kind of loneliness when a parent loses an only child. Of course, every child is unique, even in a large family. Yet there is a particular pathos about losing the only child.

This woman was a widow. That gave her an added aloneness. The loss of a child can pull parents together when both of them are living. They can cling to each other. They have another who shares the depth of their sorrow. In this case, however, the woman was experiencing her second loss. Her husband had died earlier. Now her only son was gone.

There are several lessons for our lives here. The first is that if we are going to be authentic with people, we have to try to really enter into the cost of their sorrow. Glib and superficial condolences are a waste of breath. There is a real price to be paid for genuineness. It is emotional involvement.

The second lesson is that we can identify genuineness in others by the price they are willing to pay to really care about another's hurt. A friend who is authentic in his care for us is a treasure to be valued above riches.

Power Over Death

When Jesus saw the situation He said to the corpse, "Young man, I say to you, arise." When we are dealing with a situation about which we have no confidence we qualify and hedge our statements. We say things like, "Our baseball team will win the league this year *if our pitching holds up.*" "I'm going to make a B average *if I can just keep my algebra grade up.*" We take care not to make unqualified statements.

In contrast Jesus spoke with simple authority, "Arise." There was no qualification in which He could have taken refuge if the young man had stayed dead. There was no way Jesus could save face if nothing happened. With His genuineness, though, He was not trying to hedge His statement or save face. He was willing to encounter death in the glare of the public eye. There was nothing phony about Him.

When Jesus said, "Arise," the dead man sat up and began to speak. There was a decisive response to real power. There was no beating around the bush. There was no rationalization. There was no explanation. There was only one thing, a decisive power over death clearly demonstrated.

That means to us that Jesus is able to conquer death also in our lives. We do not need to live in the shadow of our mortality. We can live freely and unafraid because our lives are committed to the One who has stood toe to toe with death and has won. Not only did Jesus raise the son of the widow of Nain, but He faced His own death and emerged from it victorious.

One of the greatest powers a man can have today is being unafraid of death. He can make decisions daringly. He can live with bracing stimulation and awesome integrity. It gives him a decided edge over others who tiptoe timidly through life trying to protect themselves from mortal dangers.

This, of course, does not suggest that we should rashly risk our lives. Jesus did not do that. It simply means that we should not allow our lives to be haunted by a specter of fear that makes us run from shadows and cower before challenges.

Seized by Fear

When people observed Jesus' power over death they had a strange reaction. They were seized by fear and glorified God. They were glad and afraid. They were elated, but unable to adjust to all the implications of the situation.

We are like that when we see something that disturbs our presuppositions. Even if something results in good news, we are disturbed if we feel that we are in the presence of a power we don't understand or can't control.

These people responded by saying, "A great prophet has arisen among us!" This appears to be an attempt to explain, more to themselves than to anyone else, why Jesus could have such power. When there is something that frightens us we want to label it, explain it. Once we have it in a pigeon hole it will not frighten us so much.

If we observe this story carefully it will remind us to open our own eyes to the working of God in unexpected ways in the world. Sometimes we have presuppositions about life that restrict our comprehension of what God can do. When that is the case we might reject or be frightened by His work. There is no need to be afraid of what God is doing. God is thoroughly good and does only good. He is thoroughly kind and acts only in kind ways. Therefore we can safely open our eyes to all of the goodness and all of the kindness that is taking place in the world.

Sometimes people are frightened by good work that is done by those who wear other religious labels. They need not be. No good work ever needs to be in competition with any other good work. No good work ever needs to be opposed by any child of God. In our lifetimes there will be many things that we do not fully understand. It is a safe rule of thumb, however, that we can be thankful for all things which produce good fruit.

The Report Spread

This message could not be contained. Soon all Judea and the surrounding country knew about Jesus and His power over death. It is the nature of news to spread.

That teaches us something about the gospel being good news. The gospel is not intended to be reduced to a set of religious platitudes and recited to captive audiences. It is intended to be told excitedly as authentic good news. Evangelism, whether public or private, does not consist in the delivering of canned speeches about religion. Our attempts to do that are usually embarrassing and ineffective in leading people to Christ.

When, however, we discover someone who is struggling under a burden of guilt and we give him news about how that burden can be cast off, the entire picture changes. We are responding in love to a person with news that he really needs to hear. We are being real and treating our friend as real. Under these circumstances the gospel is really news. It will be heard. It will spread into all the surrounding country.

Validation

A lot of frauds are passed off for genuine articles. Therefore we have developed some ways of checking to see if something is authentic. We can check to see if a twenty dollar bill is counterfeit or real. We have ways of determining whether a stone is a real diamond or an imitation one. We can check to see if a piece of jewelry is real gold or only has the appearance of it.

We further have ways of identifying people. The description on a driver's license tells height, weight, date of birth, color of hair, and color of eyes of the driver. Some have a picture of the individual. It's easy to tell whether a driver who presents that license is the actual person to whom the license was issued.

John the Baptist wanted to know whether Jesus was the authentic person or not. He wanted to know whether Jesus was the Christ or just another imitation. There had been many impostors who had already been around. John sent some people over to check Jesus out. "Are you or are you not?" they asked Jesus. As far as we know Jesus did not immediately answer a single word. He just cured diseases, cast out evil spirits, and restored sight to the blind who were present there. Then He said, "Just go tell John what you have seen."

Action is more effective than claim. All the impostors had claimed to be the Christ. Jesus did not bother, at least in this instance, to make the claim. He simply demonstrated His mission. That's a powerful way to show genuineness.

We need to remember that action is more effective than claim in demonstrating the genuineness of our Christianity also. Instead of being quick to affirm the validity of our faith we should be inclined to say, "Just observe my life. Let that observation speak to you about whether my commitment to Christ is genuine or not."

Jesus could have cited His perfect life or His divinity for His authority. Rather He showed His compassion. "Tell John what I am doing for the lepers, the blind, the deaf, and the lame," He said.

May our own identity be verified by the mercy we show to those in need.

11

The Intruder

Luke 7:36-50 is one of the tenderest and most powerful narratives in the entire New Testament. It is a story about Jesus, a religious leader, and a prostitute. The story takes some surprising turns and concludes with a devastating indictment of self-righteousness.

Simon's Curiosity

The religious leader was Simon the Pharisee. The Pharisees prided themselves on the orthodoxy of their religious position. They sort of felt that they were the "one true church" of the day. Others, they thought, had varied in one way or another from the true teachings of God and they alone had followed God without error or bias.

Scripture Resource: Luke 7:36-50

Simon appears to have been curious about the apparent power that Jesus had. Jesus was able to attract a large crowd of followers; He was saying some things that really captured the attention of the common people of the day. Simon did not know whether Jesus was a force to be feared, to be opposed, or simply a passing fad that the populace would soon forget.

Perhaps Simon thought, "If I can have Jesus in my home, I will be able to observe him at close range. I will then be able to tell whether he has any unusual power." At any rate, Simon invited Jesus to dinner. Simon was aloof but alert. He watched Jesus closely.

The Intruder

While the dinner party was in progress a prostitute came in. She was obviously a woman of the street, one who was readily recognized as being of low morals. We can imagine that the people at the table were both shocked and uneasy at her intrusion. What was she doing there? Would she show any recognition of any of them? What was she about to do?

It was customary in those days for a host to greet his guests with certain amenities. A guest coming in from a dusty street would be greeted with a basin of water and a towel. His feet would be bathed and dried. When the host wanted to show special honor to a guest, he used a fragrant and often expensive ointment to anoint the guest's head.

This street woman went directly to Jesus and began to minister to Him. Since she was not a guest but a party crasher, she did not have access to a basin of water or a towel. She wept and washed the Lord's feet with her tears. Then, strangely, she let down her hair and began to dry His feet.

For a woman to let down her hair in public was a shameful thing. It branded her as a loose and coarse woman. Perhaps this woman felt that she was already so branded that she had nothing to lose. Perhaps she wanted so much to do something to show her gratitude to Christ that she was willing to be branded for Him. In any case she accepted the stigma in order to be able to do a loving service for Christ. She kissed His feet and anointed them with ointment.

The fact that the woman anointed the feet rather than the head of Jesus probably indicates her feeling that she was a social inferior. She did not feel worthy to anoint His head as an equal might have done. She felt worthy only to anoint His feet.

Simon's Conclusion

While all of this unusual activity was going on Simon was watching with great interest. He was experiencing a sense of relief at his conclusion that Jesus had no unusual power. What a surprise Simon had in store!

Simon reasoned, "If this man were a prophet, he would have known who and what sort of woman this is who is touching him, for she is a sinner." Simon made several quick mistakes. First he concluded that he knew more about the woman than Jesus did. He was very wrong about that.

Jesus certainly knew that she was a streetwalker. As was His custom He treated her with the love and respect that is due any human being. He did not treat anyone as valueless. He did not treat anyone with contempt. He knew the pain, the trauma, and the guilt of the woman's life, but He treated her well anyway.

Simon was wrong in supposing that he knew more about the woman than Jesus did. He was also wrong in supposing that Jesus would scorn a sinner if He knew about the sin. Further Simon was wrong in supposing that there was nothing unusual about Jesus. Jesus was so unusual that He did not fit into Simon's preconceived notion of what a prophet would be like.

So Simon's conclusion was, "I have nothing to fear

from Jesus because he does not even know what kind of a woman this is."

The Story

Jesus said, "Simon, I have a little story I want to tell you." Prior to his observations of the sinful woman, Simon would have been very wary in responding to a statement like that. By this time, however, he was smugly overconfident. "Just go right ahead, Teacher," he said.

Then Jesus told one of the simplest stories one could imagine. He told of a certain man who had two debtors. One owed him a little money and the other owed him a lot. When they were unable to pay, the man just forgave both debts. "Now which one do you suppose would have the greatest appreciation?" Jesus asked.

Simon's guard was thoroughly down now. Not only did he feel that Jesus had allowed the embarrassing attention of the sinful woman but now He had told an embarrassingly simple story and asked an embarrassingly simple question. We feel the hint of condecension in Simon's voice when he says, "The one, I suppose, whom he forgave more."

The Indictment

At this point we have one of the most blistering denunciations of self-righteousness that ever fell from the lips of Jesus. Simon's comfortable complacency was suddenly shattered in an astonishing way. This Jesus, to whom Simon had felt so superior just a few minutes before, was dissecting Simon's facade with the skill of a surgeon.

"When I came in you did not even show me common courtesy," Jesus began. "Did you bring water for my feet? Yet this woman who had no water has washed my feet with her tears. Did you provide a towel?" the Lord went on. "This woman has let down her hair in front of you and all your guests and has dried my feet with her hair.

"Where was the kiss of greeting that a gracious host gives a guest?" Jesus said. "This woman has never ceased kissing my feet.

"Did you bring oil to anoint my head? This woman, who does not feel worthy to anoint my head and who has no oil, has anointed my feet with her tears.

"In short, Simon," Jesus was saying, "she has been everything to me that you have not. She has been kind, gracious, and grateful while you have been rude and arrogant.

"Yet, this poor sinful woman knows more about the reality of forgiveness than you ever will."

What a tremendous insight Jesus gives here. The reality of God's love is not best known to the person who has the best academic knowledge of the doctrine. It is best known by the person who experiences the love of God in his own life. Those closest to God are not always those who have lived the most meticulously careful lives. Sinners, too, can draw close to God.

"Me a sinner? I think you've mistaken me for someone else."

This is not because sin draws a person closer to God. Rather the feeling of self-sufficiency which often characterizes the person who has lived a "good" life will keep him from having a deep sense of appreciation of his need for God. He may feel that he needs God a little, but he will lack the overwhelming sense of dependence that the flagrant sinner will possess.

When a person knows that his life is so bad that he cannot possibly make anything worthwhile out of it on his own, he is really able to attribute all good things to God. He does not possess the pride and smugness that will keep God at arm's length from him.

That is why, as strange as it seems at first, this streetwalker was able to get closer to God than this religious official. She knew what it meant to be picked up out of the depths of degradation. Simon did not.

Shall We Continue?

The question that comes to our minds is, "If the sinner has this advantage, why should we not commit big sins so we can get closer to God?" That is essentially the question that was asked Paul when he was teaching on this same subject. "Are we to continue in sin that grace may abound?" (Romans 6:1). His response is a very strong Greek expression that means approximately, "Absolutely not!"

We do not sin in order to get closer to God. It is essential however, for us to have a healthy awareness of the fact that we have sinned and cannot get close to God on the basis of our own goodness. When we become impressed with our righteousness, we will get farther away from God.

The fact that we may be living more religious lives than others does not infer that we have an inside tract with God. That is the mistake that Simon made. He supposed that his exemplary life was more pleasing to God than the life of the sinful woman. He did not allow for the fact that he also was sinful. Neither did he allow for the fact that she was grateful and loving while he was not.

The Promise

The beautiful promise of this passage is that even the most down and out sinner can enter the closest relationship with God. It does not matter how scandalous the sin is or how tarnished the reputation is. Neither does it matter that the sinner has quit loving himself. Jesus loved the sinful woman in this passage even when she had an extremely low opinion of herself.

The promise is to all of us. Our need for Christ in our lives is enormous. When we are not able to see our need, the danger is even greater. If we can see the need so clearly that we feel hopeless, this passage is tailormade for us. It is written to say that Jesus loves us even when our lives are totally contrary to His will.

Our need is great, but His generosity is even greater. He is gracious to forgive the worst of sins. He is willing to accept people who have trouble even accepting themselves. He is the friend of those who have no other friends. He is the companion of those who are looked down on by all others.

Our gratitude should know no bounds. We must, like this poor woman, seek opportunities to pour out our gratitude and praise to Him. Though it may involve acknowledging Him in the most embarrassing circumstances, we ought to do so freely. After all, He has committed himself to us even when we had no right to expect such love.

As a postscript, let us remember from this story the folly of self-righteousness. Compared to the righteousness of Christ, none of us are righteous at all. We have no basis for boasting about our spiritual attainments. Let us rather praise God and be thankful for His love.

12

Lord, Give Me an Aspirin

What Zaccheus wanted from Jesus we do not really know (Luke 19:1-10). What he got may well have been more than he was asking for. As chief tax collector, Zaccheus was the victim of considerable social rejection. In many cases the tax collectors extorted from the people as much money as they could and enriched their own coffers with all that did not have to be turned over to the government.

Knowing that they were thus exploited, people paid taxes belligerently. They felt fully justified in avoiding taxation in every way that they could because they felt that they were so often overcharged. Most felt that tax collectors were such cheats that it was only fair that they cheat the tax collectors when they could.

Scripture Resource: Luke 19:1-10; Mark 8:34-36

Even those tax collectors who refused to participate in such plunder were required to bear the stigma of the rest. Zaccheus, the rich and powerful chief tax collector, suffered from this reputation, although there is no indication that he was any more a cheat than anyone else who saw Jesus that day.

Zaccheus wanted to see Jesus badly. Because of his shortness he ran ahead of the crowd and climbed a tree. From his perch he would be able to get a look at Jesus. Was he just curious? Was he finding out if the Lord would prejudge him as others had? Was he hoping the Lord would give him some sort of notice? Did he want something from Jesus? We do not clearly know the answers to these questions. We do know that Zaccheus was not expecting Jesus to go to his house with him. It is completely unlikely that Zaccheus expected Jesus to offer the spiritual acceptance implicit in the statement, "Today salvation has come to this house."

Just Like Jesus

Isn't that just like Jesus? It is so like Him to give us more than we bargained for.

Zaccheus had heard of Jesus' presence in Jericho and wanted to see Him. He wasn't hiding in the tree to avoid the hatred of the crowd. Neither was he planning to jump down in front of Jesus and proclaim that all of Jericho had slandered his name. And certainly, if he had come to boast about his fantastic benevolent program, Jesus would have blasted him for his self-righteousness. But when Jesus called him, his heart overflowed with gratitude and repentance. He vowed to give half his wealth to the poor and to pay back four times what he had gained from anyone he had overcharged.

Zaccheus apparently expected little more than a passing look at Jesus, and Jesus changed his whole life.

We today still have the same kind of a problem with Jesus. There are things that we want Him to do for us. We would be quite content if He would just do them and then leave us alone. His intent for us is bigger than our awareness. He does for us more than we ask. In fact, He often does more than we even want done.

We, like Zaccheus, want a casual acquaintance with Jesus. We want to be close to Him as He passes by. We want Him to help us with our problems, heal us of our illnesses, and supply us with our wants. We do not really intend to become so involved that all of our decisions are made in light of our relationship with Him. We do not plan to relinquish entirely the control of our lives. We are willing to do some things for others but don't really have in mind completely forgetting ourselves in love and service to others.

In our sense of fragmentation, we want Jesus to put it all together. When our lives are like a jigsaw puzzle with a few pieces missing, we want Jesus to supply those pieces. When we experience an internal spiritual emptiness, we want Jesus to fill that vacuum. When we have no clear grasp of our own identity, we want Him to tell us who we are. When we feel insecure we want Him to reassure us.

Give Me an Aspirin

All these things we want from Jesus. We want pains and hungers to be relieved. We want frustrations to be eased and desires to be satisfied. He keeps telling us, "The Son of man came to seek and to save the lost." He is not satisfied to give temporary relief. He insists on redeeming the whole person.

We want strong legs. He wants us to have whole souls. We want to have pleasure. He wants us to have life.

We say, "Lord, give me an aspirin." He says, "Let me get your head on straight." We say, "Lord make us pretty good." He says, "I do not do patch up jobs. I recreate."

The prospect of having Jesus redeem your whole life is frightening. It is a little like having your crutches taken away from you. They may be comfortable and reassuring, but you will never have strong legs as long as you use them. Only when you have to walk on your own legs will they gain strength. Only when you dare to run on them will they be strong.

"I'll be all right, just give me an aspirin."

Jesus knew that we hide behind handicaps and problems. If He gives us wholeness and salvation, He takes away our hiding place. I grew up in a town and a youth culture in which academic achievement was not valued. If a youth made very good grades he was likely to be ridiculed as a teacher's pet. The "in" thing to do was just to get by, not to take school seriously, and not to put any effort into school work.

As I later went on to college I often took comfort in the fact that my earlier education had been handicapped by that climate. It was a very convenient refuge when expectations were uncomfortably high or competition was unusually stiff.

Because Jesus has made me whole I have to quit leaning on that crutch. I have to quit hiding behind my mask of weakness. I have to breathe the fresh air of life and either perform or accept the responsibility for failure. I can no longer whimper, "I am a cripple." I may have just wanted a little help on a final exam; He gave me a chance to become a full grown person. I just wanted an aspirin; He made me well.

Comfortable Sins

When Jesus comes along, it's difficult to continue making excuses. Spiritual problems we've tried to overlook suddenly loom before our eyes.

When we say or do something that really hurts somebody else, we may excuse ourselves with a statement like, "I always have had a bad temper." As long as we can rationalize that we are just that way, we do not feel obligated to do anything about it. We convince ourselves that we are helpless victims of our handicap. We find that it is comfortable to be a cripple.

Jesus says, "I am not just going to relieve your immediate discomfort, but I am also going to give you the power to gain control of your temper." He has taken away our crutch. We do not any longer have any excuse not to make the battle.

Take another case. Suppose we yield to a common temptation with the remark, "I've always had that weakness." As long as we feel that way, we do not expect better of ourselves. If we get into uncomfortable trouble as a result of our sin, we can ask Jesus to help us out of the trouble. We need not be surprised if, instead of helping us out of the trouble, Jesus helps us to overcome our weakness.

Our hiding place evaporates. We have no alternative but to learn to live like full grown men and women. We cannot any longer comfort ourselves with ideas like, "I'm little and weak. I shouldn't be expected to do much better than I am doing."

Comfortable Ignorance

The same principle applies to knowing God and His will. We may justify never doing any serious study, tuning out a sermon or discussion that requires thought, and neglecting to do serious reading in the Bible and other books. "I just never was much of a student," we may reason. "It's just too deep for me," we may plead.

As a result ignorance continues unabated year after year. This is an amazingly effective evasion of the responsibility to know. It accepts ignorance as a satisfactory state and does not expect of us the disciplines and exertions of study.

I heard a preacher one time who was ridiculing college education. He was implying that those who had not been to college had a common sense that college graduates did not possess. Two or three times he made the statement, "I'm just an old ignorant country boy."

It's true that some college graduates do not have much common sense but the ones who do not have it probably did not lose it in college. It is also true that a lot of people who have never been to college lack homespun common sense.

The danger in that statement is when it is used as an escape from the expectation to learn. Ignorance can become so comfortable that a person does not really want to be any other way. One can come to enjoy the lack of responsibility that accompanies obvious ignorance.

Expectations of Wholeness

When Jesus makes you whole, you are expected to respond to life as a whole person. No longer can you enjoy the luxury of being able to pout or complain about your handicap. You can no longer blame the problem on somebody else. You cannot expect to be treated with special privileges because you are an intellectual or spiritual cripple. You cannot expect people to tiptoe around your overly sensitive feelings because you are a weakling. All of that is over now. You are a child of God. You have been given the victory.

You can burn your crutches and step forward courageously on your own two legs. The first steps may be painful and fearful. Yet the result of being a full grown person in Christ is grander than we could have first believed.

A Joyful Reception

When Jesus spoke to Zaccheus, Zaccheus' response was to make haste to come down from the tree and to receive the Lord joyously. He could not have known fully what it would mean to have Jesus come into his life. Yet whatever it was to mean, he was prepared to experience it exuberantly.

That is a beautiful example for us also to follow. When Jesus calls us to accept the salvation which is in Him, we cannot know all that such a choice will mean. As I look back over my years as a Christian, I could not have dreamed when I first gave my life to Jesus what the implications of that decision would be. Not only that, but I cannot now know what the future holds as a child of God.

Wherever He calls us we must go. Whatever He asks of us we must do. Because He is our life and our salvation we will put Him ahead of all other considerations. We will still make mistakes but we will accept responsibility for them and will even use those in our attempts to grow up fully in Him. We will learn more and more. We will be able to do more and more. We will be able to give ourselves more fully to Him.

His discipleship is an exhilarating, bracing call. We, like Zaccheus, should make haste and receive Him joyfully.

13

Mandate to Love

Sometimes the holder of a political office will announce a course of action and cite as his authority a "mandate from the voters." What he means is that he has been elected by a large majority for the express purpose of pursuing that course of action. If he has interpreted the facts right, his authority is unchallengeable.

In Mark 2:23—3:6 Jesus gives a mandate to love. He says that the rightness of doing that which responds to human need is unchallengeable. He says that we should not get into a corner where we feel like it might be wrong to do that which is authentically loving.

A Matter of Priorities

The question came up when the disciples of Jesus

Scripture Resource: Mark 2:23—3:6

were criticized for plucking grain on the Sabbath. Jesus' response was, "Have you never read what David did when he was in need and was hungry, he and his companions: 'how he entered the house of God, in the time of Abiathar the high priest and ate the consecrated bread, which it is not lawful for anyone to eat except the priests, and he gave it also to those who were with him?' " (Mark 2:25, 26 NAS).

Note that Jesus does not invalidate either the Sabbath or the law about eating the consecrated bread. He simply says that there are situations where other needs take precedence over these regulations. Jesus is not a comfort to those who want to disregard laws and regulations for their selfish pleasure. Neither does He support the view that there are no legitimate restraints on our lives. The laws about which Jesus speaks are valid laws that were made for good purposes. They were to be respected and obeyed. Jesus himself respected and obeyed them.

Though the laws were valid and deserved obedience they were not the ultimate value. When genuine human hunger was brought into the picture it had priority over the observing of the regulations.

An *antinomian* is one who is against law. He believes that there should be no firm regulations about life. Jesus opposed this point of view. He himself was a law keeper, a law respecter. Had someone violated the Sabbath for frivolous reasons Jesus would not have defended the action.

A *legalist* is one who believes that salvation is the result of correct law keeping. He elevates the keeping of the law above all other values. He might be unloving, unmerciful, or unjust as long as he was legally correct. Jesus was not trapped by this view either. Although He respected and obeyed the law, He could put a human being's need and struggle above a legal technicality.

A simple example of this is the ambulance that exceeds the speed limit in an authentic attempt to get a seriously ill person to the hospital. Such an action is thoroughly right, but it does not infer that the speed limit is not a valid regulation or that it should not, under other circumstances, be observed.

The antinomian would conclude from the example of the ambulance that the speed limit is not binding and that he can drive any speed he wishes under any circumstances. The legalist would affirm that the ambulance should never exceed the speed limit regardless of the values at stake. Both would be wrong.

Surprisingly both would be making the same basic mistake. They would be failing to see the value priorities the Lord has given to us. Jesus did not come to destroy law but to fulfill it. Yet He also came to show us that in God's view there are even higher values than legal correctness.

The Lord of the Sabbath

Jesus is talking about those comparative values when He says, "The sabbath was made for man, not man for the sabbath; so the Son of man is lord even of the sabbath." No law takes precedence over Jesus. It is not the system that is sacred but the Savior. He, not the law, is the ultimate revelation of God.

That means that when we see a conflict between correctness and Christlikeness, we ought to follow Christ. Some would argue that there could never be such a conflict. The kind of conflict that I have in mind is the kind described in this Scripture. Genuine human need is in conflict with an express regulation.

Such a conflict might occur when parents could not work and children were hungry. It is conceivable that the only possible way to feed those children would be to steal food. It is clearly not right to steal, but in this case the hunger of the children would have to take precedence over the injunction against stealing.

When Jesus said "The sabbath was made for man, not

man for the sabbath," He was saying the law was made to serve man not to crush him. He went ahead to say "The Son of man is lord even of the sabbath." The law was given for our good. We should be law-abiding citizens. Yet we should realize that our highest authority is not the law but Christ. Should we ever encounter a conflict between the law and what is clearly the loving will of Christ we must choose Christ.

No License for Indulgence

This passage is not for rationalizing. Love is not an evasion of either law or discipline. In fact love will expect more of us than law ever could. Love calls on us to do that which is for the true welfare of the beloved without regard to our own pain or cost.

It was love, not law, that took Christ to the cross. Law could require Him to keep the Sabbath, but it could not require Him to lay down His life for others. Law could require the death of the offender, but it could not require the death of the law keeper.

Here are some rules of thumb to keep in mind:

(1) Priority judgments do not invalidate commandments. Though on one occasion plucking grain on the Sabbath was the appropriate response, that fact does not mean the Sabbath was not to be respected, as Jesus himself demonstrated.

(2) Priority judgments cannot be made on the basis of selfish indulgence. This insight is not a license for justifying selfish disregard for legal regulations.

(3) Yet, priority judgments must be made. It would be easier if we had a tidy world in which there were no priority conflicts. However, this is not the way the world is. Neither does God want us to avoid the spiritual assessments and struggles that grow out of conflict situations.

Ethical Dilemmas

In his book, *The Structure of Christian Ethics,* Joseph

Sittler has a story that puts this principle into clear focus. The story comes out of World War II. A destroyer was convoying a fleet of merchant ships when one of them was torpedoed by an enemy submarine. The captain of the destroyer was able to locate the submarine with radar and was in a position to destroy it with a depth charge. The complicating factor was that a number of survivors from the downed ship were floating in lifeboats immediately above the submarine.

If the captain destroyed the submarine, he would be responsible for the death of a number of his own men. If he took no action, the submarine would undoubtedly sink other ships. There was no fully acceptable alternative. Yet a decision could not be postponed. To neglect to act was as serious as to act wrongly.

Sittler does not reveal what choice the captain made. He does quote the captain as commenting on his decision, "One must do what one must do and say one's prayers."

In other words one must choose from the available alternatives. Life often does not allow us to linger while we wish that circumstances were different.

The available alternatives often do not have all the desirable elements on one side and all the undesirable ones on the other. Therefore we sometimes have to choose a course that involves elements that we regret. When this has to be done it should be done bravely but without an attempt to defend an undesirable action as though it were a desirable one. The fact that one must say one's prayers means that we have to acknowledge that our actions are often not good enough to reflect wholly the will of God.

We must sometimes choose an alternative that we are not fully satisfied with and pursue it with conviction. There are two things, however, that we must remember. Because we may violate a value in a particular set of circumstances never means that we can, in our own defense, deny that it is a value. If we have to steal to feed a hungry child, we cannot defend ourselves by saying it is right to steal.

Secondly, the fact that a value is authentic does not mean it will always have the highest priority. Human life, for example, is an authentic value but there are circumstances in which it is better to give up life than to hold on to it. The crucifixion of Christ was one of those occasions.

An Uncomfortable Box

Those who elevate technical correctness over caring love get themselves boxed into an uncomfortable situation. As Jesus phrased it, "Is it lawful on the sabbath to do good or to do harm, to save life or to kill?" No wonder the Pharisees could not answer. To say it is better to save life that to take it would destroy their position. To say it is better to kill than to save life is so obviously wrong that they could not bring themselves to say it.

The box that the Pharisees were in was so uncomfortable that they began to seek ways to kill Jesus. There is no way to live with truth that you refuse to acknowledge. All reason is gone out of such a situation. A blind lashing out at those who represent the truth is the only course left.

Jesus responded to their dilemma by healing the man with the withered hand. Many times we need to respond to a situation with action, not argument. Instead of multiplying words about how right a course of action is, we simply need to take that course of action. A decisive, committed move is often much more convincing than a carefully reasoned speech.

The substance of Jesus' reasoning in this passage is that it is always right to do good. Regardless of the legal entanglements we may find ourselves in, we are safe in God's sight in doing the loving thing.

It will keep us out of uncomfortable boxes if we understand that 1) all good comes from God, 2) all truth comes from God, and 3) all love comes from God. There can be no other source of these three. Regardless of how confused we may become by party labels, institutional partisanship, racial or national prejudices, or any other distorting factor, we can always do the good. We can do good to all people. We can do good under all circumstances.

This does not imply it will always be easy to perceive what the good is. Often it is most difficult. It is, however, reassuring to know that if we can discern what it is in any given situation we can be sure that it is the right thing to do.